C000090832

not
.1out
r the

legal
or
ry
s

HUT UP AND FOCUS

9 Highly Effective Time Management Habits for Entrepreneurs

© Copyright 2019

All rights reserved.

The content contained within this book may
be reproduced, duplicated or transmitted with
direct written permission from the author o
publisher.

Under no circumstances will any blame or
responsibility be held against the publisher,
author, for any damages, reparation, or monet
loss due to the information contained within t
book, either directly or indirectly.

Legal Notice:

This book is copyright protected. It is only for
personal use. You cannot amend, distribute, sell,
use, quote or paraphrase any part, or the content
within this book, without the consent of the
author or publisher.

Disclaimer Notice:

Please note the information contained within this
document is for educational and entertainment
purposes only. All effort has been executed to
present accurate, up to date, reliable, complete
information. No warranties of any kind are
declared or implied. Readers acknowledge that
the author is not engaging in the rendering of

legal, financial, medical or professional advice. The content within this book has been derived from various sources. Please consult a licensed professional before attempting any techniques outlined in this book.

By reading this document, the reader agrees that under no circumstances is the author responsible for any losses, direct or indirect, that are incurred as a result of the use of information contained within this document, including, but not limited to, errors, omissions, or inaccuracies.

Table of Contents

Introduction

A year has 365 days. Everyone knows that. There are 12 months, 52 weeks and 24 hours each day. But let's narrow it down further to just one day at a time. You have exactly 1440 minutes per day. Are you making the most of it?

Hey, Bruce, got a minute?

Yeah, sure... What is it?

Well, there you go. You just wasted a minute in random chit-chat about who Kevin from HR is currently dating.

Tell us this: Did that piece of information add any value to your work? Did it affect your life in some manner? Did it excite or sadden you for some reason? Probably not, unless the one who Kevin was leaving with happens to be your partner.

Jokes apart, the one minute you wasted is something you will never get back. Do you know how much happens in a minute? According to a report by MSN, McDonald's sells over 4,500 burgers a minute, 9,700+ Ubers are booked and 590+ iPhones are sold in a minute worldwide. It puts your gibberish chit-chat to shame, no?

For any entrepreneur, time is of the essence. So you just had an idea, you worked upon it, and now you are finally earning a handsome income. Is that all you aspire to be? Is that all you ever wanted to be? If yes, then you have to drop this book right now and be on your way.

If not, then this will help you do something more. Something that will help you rise in both rank and the eyes of your loved ones. And believe me, there is no secret to it. It is all about managing your time and priorities. One thing even Elon Musk struggles with.

A lot of time is wasted every day doing unproductive work. Work that doesn't bring in any sales, work that doesn't contribute to your health or leaves you with having to compromise on other important areas of your life—your family. If you are one of those entrepreneur dads or partners who is always late to a party or, worse, don't make it just because you are juggling with so much on your plate and don't have time for you or the kids, then this book is for you.

It is also for you if you or your business has been suffering and you keep wondering what you could have done better to improve your sales or generate more profits. It is common knowledge that most of the things we do at the last minute aren't as well thought-out and research-oriented. Think about the last time you went last-minute shopping for Christmas for someone you love. Was your instinct to get them something thoughtful or just get them 'anything' so that you don't have to show up empty-handed? The last-minute tasks are never the best and hold little value. The same applies to business. Anything hasty and conceived at the last minute doesn't hold the appeal something planned does. What delays things is the lack of time. The more time we have to plan things, the more thorough and involved we are. The best outputs and outcomes result where there hasn't been an opportunity cost to pay.

So if it all comes down to time, don't you think you need to learn to manage it?

A normal person's day is broken down into time segments. You need to get to work by a certain time, get to the bank within a specified set of operating hours, go to the grocery, fetch your kids from school and watch them.

Depending on the type of business you own, you may need to speak with clients, set up meetings, finish products, ship them out, etc. Entrepreneurs fulfill a lot of roles in their businesses, and it is very easy to let one task overwhelm the others. This can translate to lost income—because the entrepreneur may end up missing something vital.

You may feel like you never seem to get enough done in a day, that you are always running after something. If you are already knee-deep in your business, you may feel like the clock is running after you.

You need to manage your time to get maximum returns from your mini-investments during the day. These are the minor things that you do during the day that end up adding up and give you a sense of accomplishment.

Knowing what tasks you will be doing for the day, controlling your time can reduce the amount of stress that you experience on a day-to-day basis. Even simple techniques can bring you to a point where the stress is easily managed.

So what is time management, exactly? And why do you need it in your life? Here's what I know and believe in. Managing your time is all about taking control of your life. It is about doing things with the most added value benefits at the end of the day. It is allowing yourself to follow a roadmap, ensuring that every roadblock is handled at a certain time and with efficiency.

The first thing you must remember is that time management is a skill. Great!

Unlike talents, everyone can learn a new skill. Skills are trainable. Have you ever tried your hand at something new? Perhaps, you learned a new language? Was it not difficult at first? Didn't you want to give up? But eventually, when you stuck with it, you learned it. Today, speaking that language might feel like a habit. Any new habit becomes as easy as breathing once it is practiced enough. So is the case with time management. But for every new habit, you need to get rid of the destructive ones first. Sadly, we live in an age where information and technology are linked undeniably, which leaves us with waves of knowledge that is of no use to us.

Imagine you decided to wake up early so that you can catch up on some fresh air and have more time to handle work commitments. To do that, you will need to sleep early. If you are someone who has the habit of watching TV before bed or wasting time browsing social media, you will have to give it up or else your sleep and health will be compromised. Thus, to adopt good habits, you need to forgo a bad one.

And after some time it will feel more like a lifestyle than practice, and that is the goal of this whole book.

Most entrepreneurs, like myself, have complained about a lack of time and organization. Sometimes it is their family that has to suffer and other times, the business. Since either can't be taken for granted or expected to sprout without you, your job is to find the middle ground: a way that prioritizes things in an order where nothing gets neglected. I want you to have no guilt at the end of the day. There shouldn't be an opportunity cost that you should pay just because of your lack of organization and management. Your kids shouldn't have to miss a parent on their birthday because they are stuck with some pending work that should have been completed days before.

In this book, together we shall learn about 19 such highly effective habits that are going to help you generate more revenue for your business and also give your family and friends the time they deserve. Meaning, neither of the two will have to suffer. I have personally adopted these, and I have seen the magnitude of what grander change it can bring into your life. Why do I call them highly effective, you might wonder? It is because these have proven to hold worth and allow you, as a struggling entrepreneur, to manage both your workload as well as other important affairs without looking at your watch from time to time, thinking where the hell did I waste so many hours of the day?

Each habit is simple, doesn't need a lot of effort on your part, and will be easy to adopt and live by. With these newfound habits, not only will you be able to manage your time properly, but also use that extra time to work on more income-driving habits. So this will not only free up time but make you more money in the long-term.

Let's begin!

Chapter 1: Avoid Procrastination and Finish the Most Urgent Task First

In the first chapter, we shall talk about some of the most pressing and common habits that people have. The first being procrastination and the second, wasting time doing unimportant tasks and failing to accomplish the most important ones.

The first habit that holds you back from your dreamed success as an entrepreneur is your persistence in delaying things until the last minute. You easily fall victim to the word tomorrow. Not only does that sound enticing to you, but it also serves as the wrong kind of motivation. After all, why would you want to delay doing something you can easily do today or right now?

There is some science behind it. Let's learn something about that first!

Habit #1: Avoid Procrastinating

Entrepreneurs are brilliant thinkers with an abundance of ideas, tasks, and projects. If these ideas and projects aren't in the process of implementation already, you can't expect to succeed. So let's begin by calling it an entrepreneur's biggest enemy.

The combination of the two can be deadly, and thus not advisable. In the simplest of terms, you may define procrastination as the act of delaying or avoiding doing things that need to be accomplished. Broadly speaking, it is the practice of choosing more pleasurable things over less pleasurable ones, or accomplishing the less urgent tasks in place of urgent ones—the outcome of which isn't favorable or profitable in the long run.

You might not even realize that while you are getting up for your fourth cup of coffee for the day or wasting time scrolling down your Facebook newsfeed, you are putting your business in second place and your comfort at first. No entrepreneur who does that ever achieves what they dream of. Your goals and aspirations should always be a priority.

You might think that the age of the internet is to

blame for the rise in population of procrastinators, but you are gravely mistaken. Centuries ago, 800 B.C. to be precise, Hesiod, a famous Greek poet of his time, cautioned readers to not put off important things for tomorrow. Even then, he was genius enough to notice the lazy attitude of the people. But, hey, that is just recorded history. What if procrastination existed way before that too? For all we know, the dinosaurs saw the meteorite coming toward them but went back to eating and BAM!

The reason I want to stress this is that not only is procrastination detestable, it is also downright harmful. Studies have proven that procrastination leads to increased levels of stress and reduced well-being (Eerde, 2016). True procrastination is the prime failure of self-regulation. Things don't just randomly get delayed. You have a voluntary role to play in the postponement. Although a poor time concept exacerbates the problem, the poor management of emotions or, to put it better, lack of control over your emotions seems to be the core problem.

There are two schools of thought regarding procrastination. One school regards it as harmful and hateful, while the other looks at it as a positive motivator. The sympathizers believe that the delay in accomplishing tasks can serve as beneficial in helping the doer sort out between the most and less urgent ones. And as long as the important ones get done, it doesn't matter how much time they took. They go as far as calling it working your best under pressure. John Perry, a Stanford philosopher, in his book called The Art of Procrastination finds it crucial to your success. However, he stresses that one must reassess their list of to-dos when short on time and give their fullest to the most important tasks at hand first.

Psychological scientists, on the other hand, find it problematical. They believe that the act of delaying things until the very last minute conflates proactive behaviors as well as the art of prioritizing and replaces it with detrimental and self-defeating habits.

Keeping all that in mind, have you ever thought why do you procrastinate?

Is there some trigger(s)? If so, what could they be?

Why are we obsessed with the word "Tomorrow"?

Here are some of the reasons I believe contribute toward the profound admiration for delaying work.

No concrete goals

Having a vague or abstract goal just makes the whole idea of working less interesting (McCrea, Liberman, Trope, & Sherman, 2008). The lack of knowledge or perhaps a vision can make you want to put it off. For instance, you may have decided to start meditation but that is just a vague goal unless you know what you wish to achieve with it. Is it more clarity of your thoughts that you seek or just a clutter-free paradigm to seek new information. Unless you are clear on your goals, you are less likely to take it up. The same applies to tasks.

Hoping For a better option

Another reason why entrepreneurs delay their tasks in the present is that they see a more hopeful and viable option to perform it shortly. It may work in cases where the present lacks the resources and set of skills required, but it fails at some point. It leads to long-term procrastination, which is even worse. Most of the time, the individual just delays the task and ends up with no intended course of action.

Indecisiveness

Sometimes, entrepreneurs procrastinate because they think they are bad at making decisions on time (Tibbetta & Ferrarib, 2015). The delay occurs because the individual wastes too much time in identifying which course of action will be the most profitable and beneficial. The lack of decisiveness just puts things on hold until the very last minute. For instance, you might have a ton of ideas for your next sales campaign, but you might not be able to pick one. The abundance of choices and your inability to categorize them in the order of most beneficial to least beneficial will make the task stressful and tedious.

Distractions

Distraction and procrastination are friends for life. They go hand in hand, scouting on vulnerable entrepreneurs who give in quickly. The moment they spot their prey, they make sure the job is well done. Distraction makes other tasks more interesting than the one at hand. It could be a beeping message, a delightful snacking session or just watching out of your window looking at strangers.

The more distracted you are, the less likely you are to complete an unfinished task and add to your tomorrow's to-do list.

Doubts about control

Sometimes, entrepreneurs procrastinate because

they are doubtful about the outcomes of their choices as they hold no control over the input. For instance, you might not want to start on a project that you already know won't get approved or appreciated. No matter how much you try, you just know that you won't be able to accomplish it and that low self-regard leads to procrastination.

Aversion toward tasks

Often the tasks that we don't feel excited about are delayed for a later date in the future. Task aversion is a common yet ignored phenomenon. The majority of us complete tasks because we have to and not because we like to. That very difference is what makes us delay it till the very last minute. Picture this, you need to make an important phone call to someone you know you can't stand. Would you delay it or get it over with. Your first natural response would be to delay it because it doesn't excite you. The more unappealing the task, the lesser chances of it reaching completion.

Perfectionism

When people aim for perfection, they become extremely cautious and self-critical (Pychyl & Flett, 2012). This also becomes one of the reasons for procrastination. You might be so afraid of making a mistake that you might put off trying it all together. The idea of flawing build too much pressure that you become anxious whenever there is a mention of it.

Sensation Pursuing

Lastly, some people also procrastinate because they want to make the task more challenging, add some excitement to it and see how well they do it under pressure (Piers, 2007).

You may have to deliver a presentation to potential clients the following day and you don't start working on it until the night because you want to see if you are strong enough to take up the challenge and risk your chances of success with the newfound thrill plus anxiousness. You may have delayed it because it seemed uninteresting before that and you didn't feel like wasting your time over it.

In some rare cases, it may work out well for you once but it won't all the time. Add to that the additional stress you will experience that may very well hinder your performance while delivering the presentation even though you had it all sorted in your head and on the screen.

Lack of motivation

Another significant reason we procrastinate is that we aren't driven enough to work on a task. We lack the required motivation. When we were growing up, most of the things we did were because we were pressured into doing them. We cleaned our plates, we made our bed, and we went to sleep before midnight. Why? Because we were extrinsically motivated by our parents. Extrinsic motivation is similar to a lack of motivation because there is no intrinsic will to accomplish a task. When we suffer from a lack of motivation or motivated extrinsically, we are likelier to procrastinate (Katz, Eilot, & Nevo, 2014).

Requiring instant gratification

Many of us like to live in the present. Although a monk will tell you of the countless benefits of living in the present, it doesn't work very well when it breeds unhealthy and harmful habits such as procrastination. We all crave instant gratification. We want the results of our marketing campaigns right away. We want to know how well we do in the last quarter even when the next one has just begun. We want to know exactly how much we will be made before the end of this year.

The point being, we are more excited about trying things with an instant reward attached to it. Sometimes it is monetary and most of the time—intangible. Watching meaningless TV will always feel better than working on an Excel Spreadsheet. We prioritize things linked with some short-term gratification and thus procrastinate over things with long-term value. Why? It is because watching TV is more pleasurable in the present.

From procrastinator to productive, knocking out the enemy

Now that we have all the reasons jotted down in our minds, we need to move onto the solution. How can one overcome procrastination and whether if it is an achievable task or not?

Habits are changeable suggests psychology. It may take you some time to overcome something detrimental, but you will eventually overcome it. Sooner than you know, it will feel like a part of you and become natural. I have broken down the process in a few steps, each with a promising potential to get you off your seat and attend to all the pending tasks at once.

Have clearly-defined deadlines

Deadlines are what push us forward. The sooner

the deadline, the harder we work. When I started writing this book, I was juggling between two different businesses and my family. Of course, there were setbacks, lack of ideas and low levels of motivation, but the day I assigned myself a deadline to finish it, it changed the whole scenario. I felt more driven, deliberately avoided distractions and set a time to work on the book every day for two hours. Previously, I had no track of where I spent had the 24-hours and doing what, but with a deadline in place, everything changed. I was more cautious about the time spent on each task during the day so that I could go home and work on the book. The result of it is in your hands right now.

Deadlines, whether set by a client or yourself, can significantly boost your productivity an interest in the task.

Coming to the second more crucial aspect of the heading is setting a deadline that isn't too far-fetched. You must have one that is near so that you avoid any chance of falling under the spell of procrastination. The sooner a deadline, the bigger the urgency to complete it.

Break down your goals

You can't achieve everything overnight, so try not

to. Each task, whether big or small, requires focus and determination. Having too much on your plate will only lead to confusion, increased stress and fear of failure—the perfect recipe to procrastinate. However, when you break down your goals into achievable milestones, that's a whole different story. You set a fixed time to start on one task and take it to completion with all your might and focus. These little bouts of accomplishments will further oomph your motivation, and once that adrenaline kicks in it's like kryptonite for procrastination.

Stay sane and don't multitask

Multitasking keeps the mind distracted. It may work for some but if you come to think about it, divided attention didn't get anyone any good. You work your best when you are focused on a particular task and putting all your mental and physical efforts toward its completion. When you have too much occupying your mind, there is a possibility that you might want to just give up everything and put it all on hold because it feels too chaotic in your head.

Thus, if the goal is to avoid delaying things, stay focused on just one at a time and give your 100% to it.

Set rewards for your accomplishments

Positive Reinforcement isn't just for pets. Have you ever wondered how did we come up with the concept in the first place? Positive reinforcement works for everyone: kids, teenagers, adults, and seniors. Rewards boost performance as one can convince their mind that something good is going to happen. The same works for procrastination.

Setting rewards for the competition of several tasks is more likely to make you want to complete them. It could be as little as going home an hour early or as big as taking the entire weekend off to visit the beach. The key is to keep you focused on the task and prevent procrastination.

Keep work hours short

Long work hours not only saturates the mind, but it also diminishes our excitement and motivation toward completing a task. This leads to procrastination. Thus, taking short breaks between the tasks is ideal as it keeps your mind refreshed. When the mind is revitalized, even the most mundane of tasks seem doable. For an aspiring entrepreneur, this is highly crucial as motivation is imperative when starting to turn dreams into a reality.

Moreover, during your break time, try not to think about the task. Utilize that time to perform some mental exercises or chit-chat. Constantly, thinking about the task will only make it seem harder and less enjoyable—this makes you procrastinate.

Habit # 2: Finish the Most Important Task First

If you have an important task scheduled for the next day, aim to do it first thing in the morning. Several studies propose that accomplishing the most important tasks first leaves one with a sense of accomplishment, satisfaction, and even joy. It enhances productivity and also boosts confidence. Ernest Hemingway worked on his writing first thing upon waking up. According to him, it happens to be the most peaceful time of the day and there is no disturbance to abrupt the flow of writing. His story and many other similar stories of famous authors, entrepreneurs, athletes, and actors are quoted in Daily Rituals: How Artists Work by Mason Currey (Currey, 2013). It is a great read if you are fascinated with how your inspirational idols do things.

If there is a correlation with productivity and accomplishment of important tasks, shouldn't you, as an entrepreneur, who has a million things to accomplish in the limited number of hours, learn it and swear by it for eternity?

Yes, I thought so too!

Well, I am going to be straightforward with you here. The tip is nothing but trying to accomplish the most important or urgent task first thing in the morning. Like any other entrepreneur, you must have a to-do list for the day. On that list, there must be some tasks requiring urgency, some tasks that aren't that urgent and some that can be scheduled for a less hectic day.

If you have the approach of ticking all of them off in a single day, great. In a hypothetical world, it will work. In the real world, however, you will always be running short of time, no matter how hard you try. Thus, an ideal approach should be to try to accomplish the ones that require urgency first. Failing to do so will leave you with a mix of some important and unimportant tasks accomplished with some of both remaining. Imagine, if you got all the unimportant tasks accomplished and fell short on completing any of the ones near a deadline? You don't want to be in that fix now, do you?

Identify any three to five MITs that you must, no matter what, complete by the end of this working day. Even if you have, say 15 to-dos on your list, you would still have at least three or five completed.

On the other hand, if you multitask and spend your time, effort and resources tackling, say 10 in a day, you might only complete a few and still have many incomplete. Which approach do you think will make you feel more accomplished and proud?

Why does it work?

To some entrepreneurs, productivity is getting a lot done in a day. For some, it is getting things done consistently. The first entrepreneur is concerned with the numbers on the spreadsheet, whereas the other one focuses on consistency in those numbers. Both these mindsets have their pros and cons, but I live by the second approach. I aim for steady progress, even if it means less work. Achieving speed isn't my biggest goal, but rather progressing continuously. Do you see the difference? I am more concerned with whether I am moving any closer to my goals or just handling each obstacle as it comes.

To put this into practice, I tackle the most important task first thing each day. Sadly, I learned this the hard way. There were days when I spent the most crucial hours of my day ticking off the 3rd, 4th, or 5th task on my to-do list instead of accomplishing the important ones. It took me time to realize that not only did I need to reorder my to-do list, I also needed to get the most important ones out of the way first.

Why you may ask? Look at the remarkable benefits:

Crowning willpower

It is proven by science that our decision-making ability and willpower are the highest first thing in the morning. As the day passes, we see a decline in both and thus might end up making poor decisions. Knowing that, wouldn't it be best if you get done with the most important task first?

Fewer distractions

Morning is a peaceful time. You have just woken up, haven't had to go through the nerve-wracking traffic or listened to your secretary dictate your schedule for the day. And the biggest perk... There are no emails whatsoever waiting to be checked, replied to, or spammed. Now correct me if I am wrong and suggest you tackle MITs first thing.

Builds Impetus

MITs are usually the most boring and challenging tasks. Getting them off of your to-do list will leave you with the less important or boring ones. Besides, when you are done with the bigger chunk, the smaller ones seem easier and accomplishable. There is a chance that you may end up completing more than you had anticipated.

How does it work?

Makes sense, no? But how will it play out in reality? Great, you have made up your mind to work on MITs but how do you identify one from the uncountable tasks on your to-do list? Here's a simple formula that I follow. There are only three steps to it, and each will take you less than a minute to sort through.

The 3-minute Trick to Identify MITs

Step 1: Start With a Second List

Not a second list but making another smaller one from the one you already have. A lot of times we overestimate the number of tasks we can accomplish in a day. Generally, there are 3-5 tasks one can feasibly accomplish in a day. So what are the top priority tasks that you wish to get down with by the end of the day? Knowing that is the first step.

Step 2: List them by Order of Urgency

The second step involves organizing those tasks in a sequence. Which task has the most beneficial outcome? Arrange them by order, and you now have an order in place to start working with.

Step 3: Just Do It

Not technically a step, the goal is to start right away. Start from the top and work your way through. Don't skimp on things or try to multitask. Only move forward once you are done with the task at hand.

Chapter 2: Handling Emails and Saying No When Appropriate

It's Monday again. As you sit at your desk you sense a sinking feeling in your stomach. You know that the moment you open your laptop, you will be flooded with hundreds of emails just waiting to be opened.

If you are in charge of a large team, chances are that you will easily receive 10-plus emails first thing in the morning. Been there and done that, as they say. Going through each, sorting them, responding to them, forwarding some to others just seems like it's going to take all day.

And then a thought hits you... You didn't become an entrepreneur just so you would be bombarded with emails all day. You became an entrepreneur so that you could head a successful business. But what about the inbox and those pending ones from yesterday and the day before that? What about all those emails that need to be responded too?

What if there weren't any? Hypothetically speaking, what if there was a world where there were no emails to be sent, forwarded, or replied to?

Well, why hypothetically?

In this chapter, we are going to aim to get your email list to a zero. We will talk about the different techniques you can use to prevent the bombardment of emails and, more importantly, stop them from piling up.

Secondly, we shall talk about another damaging habit that entrepreneurs have—saying yes to things that aren't important. We shall learn to say no and also why it is crucial for you and your business's growth.

Habit 3: Getting Your Email List Down To a Zero

To achieve success, you first need to know the definition of the word success. Similarly, if you want to achieve a zero inbox, you need to understand what it truly means. The term inbox zero was coined by Merlin Mann, productivity guru. Despite common belief, it has nothing to do with the number of emails you have in your inbox, instead, it is about regaining control over the monotonous practice of email checking.

Most of us spend a good amount of hours checking emails and responding to them. Even when it isn't a part of our job description, we are accustomed to checking them periodically in case something of top priority comes along and requires action. And in case we get busy elsewhere, there is a pile waiting to greet us the next time we go online. The piling of unanswered emails can stress you out in no time.

If a majority of your emails begin with "Sorry for the late reply," then it means you have a problem that needs to be resolved.

Why Achieving a Zero Inbox is Crucial?

But why is it this crucial and what good comes

from it? For starters, an inbox zero relieves you from the stress of wasting important time that can be utilized elsewhere.

Even when there isn't any email requiring an urgent response, they still need to be backlogged for future references. According to research, this can cause a psychological drag. This means that we lose mental focus and clarity.

Secondly, when we are checking our emails, we have the habit of opening at least three to seven before actually taking action on one of them. This practice not only delays response time but also adds to your stress in case a new email pops-up. Once you are done replying to it, you go back to each open tab and reread the email, losing precious time.

A zero inbox eliminates this waste of time and helps you to learn how to go through each message just once. This leaves you more time to be productive in other areas of your work and also meet deadlines.

Next, with an inbox zero, you don't overlook any important emails and they surely don't get buried in the pile of reading emails. You achieve this by sorting out each email in separate folders based on their urgency, whether they need to be addressed or not, or do they need to be saved as a reminder for some later date or not.

This way, even if your mind fails to recall an important task you were emailed about, you can always go back to the folder you placed it into and remember it in less than a minute.

A zero inbox also prevents procrastination, which is again a possibility when you have too much on your plate. We discussed earlier how an overload of work can demotivate one to start. It happens with an overcrowded inbox as well.

Finally, when you achieve a zero inbox, there are no pending unread emails in your inbox. Can there be any relief bigger than that?

Zero Inbox and Improved productivity?

On average, an entrepreneur is exposed to 126 emails per business day (sent and received) in 2019. Among these, many need to be responded to urgently. Moreover, the same study also reveals that we spend approximately 11 hours per week sending and receiving emails (Email Statistics Report, 2015-2019, 2015).

Although designed as a productivity enhancer, email reading can sometimes become a source of distraction and loss of focus. Did you know it takes a person about 23 minutes to get back to the work they were doing after responding to an email? If you are constantly wasting that much time after every email, how are you going to get any work done at all during the day? Despite trying to avoid the "bing" of a new email or a pop-up on your desktop, we just can't resist the temptation of opening it, can we? In a way, we are a lot like Pavlov's dogs who were conditioned to salivate when the bell rang. Even when we know that in doing so we are deliberately making our minds suffer the psychological drag and waste time.

It's Difficult but Possible

If you are aware of Greek mythology, you must know the Hydra. The magnificently scary creature with nine snakeheads—cut off one and in its place grow two heads. Managing an inbox today is similar to battling a nine-headed Hydra. Every time you think addressing this last unread mail will free you up, two more come along popping.

So maintaining a zero inbox seems quite difficult but not impossible. Hey, if Hercules can do it, so can you! Here's how you are going to succeed at it.

Assess Your Inbox

First, just take a clear and thorough look at what's in front of you. Don't touch or open or address any email, just browse through the list, dates, sender and subject lines. Once you have a mental note prepared, ask yourself the following questions.

- What type of emails are you receiving the most? Is it junk mail, messages from social networking sites, newsletters from subscribed websites, or messages from the boss or colleagues?
- What is the date you received them? Are they months old or just arrived a few hours back?
- Who's repeatedly messaging you? You must have some regulars who keep asking about every little detail.
- What are the subject lines like? Are they offering info right away or luring you with click-bait titles?

This identification will not only help you with the organization of your inbox but also help you develop a plan of action on which to address first and how. Furthermore, it will help you recognize where you're lacking and help you fix it. For example:

- If you receive more junk mail, then it is a priority issue.
- If you receive emails from one or two senders only then it is a communication issue.
- If you receive most emails on Monday, then it is a scheduling issue.

Unsubscribe and Spam

The next and most important step to achieving a zero inbox is spamming and unsubscribing to emails that are nothing but time-wasters. It will take a few hours to get the job done, but it will save you hours moving forward. The clutter needs to go so that you are left with a less stress-causing inbox and deliver timely responses and use the remaining time to work on MITs.

Here are examples of some of the types of emails that you must receive regularly.

1. Emails from colleagues and clients
2. Emails from customers and well-wishers
3. Emails from people you never respond to
4. Newsletters
5. Social media alerts

For managing the first three categories, use folders and labels. Folders and labels allow you to easily sort your emails and reach out to them immediately when needed. When naming your folders, be very thorough as you don't want to make it yet another unmanaged folder like your inbox.

For every email that you receive, whether from your clients, customers or well-wishers, ask yourself if you need to address them immediately or not. Next, decide on a course of action. If you don't plan to respond to it right away but say you will in a few hours, place it in the folder titled, "Need to respond to."

If you think that waiting a little longer, say days or weeks, won't make any difference, place it in a different folder titled, "Respond Later." If you have the time, let the sender know that you plan on responding but would appreciate some more time.

The last two categories can also be managed using the same technique; however, I want you to have full control over them and come out as a conqueror. Remember, we are trying to defeat the Hydra here?

Newsletters

You might not even remember when and how did you subscribe to them. Of course, they are from websites you know or stores you love to visit but why do they keep sending you this newsletter about how well they did in the last quarter, what new things are happening at their end and what new products are being promoted.

If you ask me honestly, I will tell you to unsubscribe to all of them right away but before I turn into the bad guy here, you need to ask yourself three questions to decide their fate.

- How often are they opened by you?
- How often do you read them after opening them?
- How often do you use them? Do you save it for later reading, but what they are promoting or write down the coupon numbers for future use?

If you don't have an answer to any of these, unsubscribe and delete it. If you love the brand/business, you are going to buy from them, with or without a reminder from them.

Social Media Alerts

This is a combination of emails you receive from your social media accounts in case you use the same email ID to log in on them. These include emails from Facebook, YouTube, Twitter, Instagram, Spotify, Skype, Pinterest, Snapchat, Medium, LinkedIn, etc. A majority of these just remind you of redundant information as someone commented on your post or your tweet was retweeted this many times, etc.

For starters, if you are managing a business, it is best to keep your professional and private IDs separate. If you can't, as so many people now have this ID as the only means of a link to you, go into the settings of each of these social apps and turn off the email alerts.

Habit 4: Learn to Say NO to Things That Add No Substantial Value

Don't kids love to say the word no to everything? Honey, finish your vegetables. NO! Wake up, it's time for school. NO! We have to go to the doctor's appointment. NO! It's time for you to stop playing and go to bed. NO!

It seems effortless, right? It's because they are solely concerned about what they want and how they feel. And then we are introduced to all these emotions, feelings, and thinking about others' crap. Well, technically not crap but saying yes to everything does complicate things, doesn't it?

As we grow older, the word "no" seems like a distant memory and "yes" becomes the order of the day. No day goes by when we don't do things just to please people. And it stems from the fact that, deep down, we all want to be liked and appreciated by others. So we end up doing things that we wouldn't have initiated on our own had someone not asked us to do.

For an entrepreneur or magnate, whose primary job includes persuading others to buy their products or services, people-pleasing is an important skill to have. It's because you are risking your stakes in the hope of earning some profits and to do that, you have to chase after every opportunity that comes along the way. And how do you do that? By engaging in contact with others, offering a few favors here and there and other similar modes of convincing. This strategy does work when you are just starting, but after some time you might find yourself overcommitted and exhausted.

What we entrepreneurs forget sometimes is that doing business isn't a race. It involves working smart and not just hard. Your time is valuable and thus should only be utilized on things posing utmost urgency and enticing revenues. Therefore, saying no to things that don't add any value whatsoever to your life or business is not just acceptable but a necessity.

Why Entrepreneurs Love the Word "Yes"

To learn how to say no, we must first learn why we say yes so often? More importantly, why is our thought process?

Studies reveal that there are several reasons entrepreneurs just can't risk saying no.

- Entrepreneurs are chasers: Entrepreneurs are chasing after opportunities all the time. After all, what's the point of running a business if you aren't doing that, right?

This is one reason why they always find themselves double or triple booked.

- Entrepreneurs are hard to please: Since they are thinkers and doers, they are always thinking about the "What's next." They are never content with what they have, and they are always looking for ways to do things better.

- Entrepreneurs are risk-takers: Again, true. That is the whole point of building an empire. They are more likely to dive into projects quickly and thus often end up with more than what they bargained for.

Why You Must Excuse Yourself?

Although it may seem hard to turn down something of value, there are some side-effects of overbooking yourself on tasks and projects. The truth is, there's always a limit to what you can do and failing to meet the committed deadlines will only harm your rapport with clients and customers. Moreover, you will waste valuable time doing something that doesn't have a promising return and feels burnt out. An exhausted businessman is no use to anyone.

Furthermore, if you don't say no to things that don't guarantee a substantial advantage, you risk losing your focus. Becoming a people pleasure

46

can land you in shallow waters as you may make decisions that benefit no one—not your company, employees, or yourself. A lack of focus will havoc your business standing and you may even fail to meet your original goals.

Have you ever met someone who builds a business around someone else's idea or suggestions? How well did they do? Your ideas fuel your business. You can never be a successful entrepreneur if you aren't passionate about the thing you do. It has to come from within you. Thereof, say no when required, without feeling guilty because at the end of the day, it is your investment, efforts, resources and time.

How to Say No To Things with No ROI?

The majority of entrepreneurs rush headstrong into the business world with a to-do list and tons of expectations. Coming armed like this makes it difficult to say no. What they need is a to-don't-do list so that they can make wiser decisions. The key here is to learn when it is okay to say no and when letting go is the best option. Here are some great ideas to put into practice to get you started on this new journey of saying no.

Seek Answers from Within You

Time is the most precious of resources and a

successful entrepreneur knows that. The bigger you get, the more people you will come across seeking favors and requests. If you have a difficult time deciding and evaluating whether to say yes to their request or not, ask yourself these important questions listed below. Believe me, you will have your answer in no time.

1. Does it benefit your company's image?
2. Does it excite you?
3. Do the efforts outweigh the outcomes?
4. What is your gut feeling about it?
5. It is aligning with your core business objectives?

If you mentally answered yes to all these, you know it is a task worth taking. If any of the projects you take up don't drive your business toward success, are they worth investing your time in?

In the words of Adam Grant, a bestselling author, and professor, "Saying no frees you up to say yes when it matters most." (Grant, n.d.)

Change your attitude

Aspiring entrepreneurs often have a scarcity mindset. They think that if they say no to any opportunity coming their way, it may never come again. The worst thing about this kind of mentality is that you also end up saying yes to clients who aren't worthy or a good fit. Suppose you fail to meet their expectations due to overload at work, not only did you waste your time on them, but you also have to live with a bad word of mouth through them. Thus, opt for an abundance mindset instead. The abundance mindset suggests that good clients are abundant out there, you just need to wait until you find them or they find you and save your best for them.

Aim for focus

Steve Jobs, in an Apple Worldwide Developers Conference, once said, "People think focus means saying yes to the thing you've got to focus on. But that's not what it means at all. It means saying no to the hundred other good ideas that there are. You have to pick carefully. I'm as proud of the things we haven't done as the things I have done. Innovation is saying no to 1,000 things."

This means that you have to be wise to choose the things you want to invest your time into. Sometimes, you just have to be a ruthless time manager. This is important because only when you value your time, you will be able to focus on the more important tasks and prioritize them. After all, they are what will take your business forward and help you achieve your long-term goals.

When you say no to unwanted clutter, you are saying yes to more important goals by reserving your time and mind for them.

Chapter 3: Dealing with Time Wasters and Living by the 80/20 Rule

In chapter 3, we shall learn about what time wasters are, how to overcome them and what does it mean to live by the 80/20 rule for an entrepreneur. Most entrepreneurs struggle when it comes to prioritizing their tasks and end up wasting precious time over unnecessary time wasters. To help you, choose better and wiser, you must first learn what they are and whether you have been indulged in them without intention or knowledge.

Habit 5: Dealing with Time-Wasters

What is a time-waster, exactly?

A time-waster is anything or anyone that detracts, distracts, distances or diverts your attention from something important such as your plans, appointments, events, goals or activities. Sometimes they are self-made and thus self-destructive. If I were to describe time waster as a person, I would call them smart. They lure you into their charm so effortlessly that you don't even realize where the time went by. It's like sitting through a really good opera concert and losing yourself completely in the aura and magic. However, the end isn't quite as applaud-able as you may feel frustrated, stressed, or overwhelmed afterward.

Time wasters also come in different forms and shapes. They can be a task, the environment, an appointment, a location, activity or someone you know.

No matter how much you enjoy indulging in them, they aren't good for the business. Lucky for you, they are predictive and thus, preventable. They can be controlled with better though processing and quick responding. Take a look at some of the most common time wasters in the life of an entrepreneur.

The 6 Most Common Time Wasters

1. Social Media Surfing

The biggest and most annoying time-waster is browsing the internet. There is always something shinier than the last picture, like a bigger diamond in the mine. Like most people, entrepreneurs too innocently waste too much time surfing the web, wasting time on a website unrelated to work. Social media not only distracts one from important work, but it also becomes a source of procrastination. You keep telling yourself that you will get back to work when the clock hits a certain time, but it never really happens. The next time you look up at your clock, the set time has already passed and you have no choice but to allow yourself a new time to close all those enticing tabs.

You must keep in mind that although it is nice to have an online presence when you are running a business, it isn't a necessity for you as the business owner. You can always delegate the job to someone to keep tabs on your business and research the needs of your customers and clients respectively. Your job is to ensure that the work gets done and the suggestions posted online are turned into a reality for better customer experience.

2. Busy Checking Messages

Checking your emails now and then chews up your time like anything. Not only that, but it also distracts you from far more important tasks. According to research, business owners check their emails 30 times per day. And since we already established that it takes one 23 minutes to get back to working again, you can imagine the amount of time lost doing meaningless work.

3. Accomplishing Routine Tasks

Many entrepreneurs, ignited by the fire of excitement, take up more than what they bargain for. They are the ones handling the finances, marketing, production, and sales of the job. It is okay to take responsibility for most things, but it is against the principle of working smart. What they don't realize is that while they are trying to multitask, they are losing enormous amounts of time doing mundane tasks that can be delegated instead.

To identify these time-wasters, make a list of all the tasks you perform in a day. Once you have the list identify all those tasks that are delegable such as running to the suppliers and getting your supplies delivered, assigning teams in the production department, managing the social media channel to answer queries, personally responding to all emails received, etc. etc.

Next, create another list of the most important tasks you must accomplish. Tasks that only you can do, tasks that require your expertise and knowledge such as dealing with clients. Do you think that there is no one capable of dealing with the routine tasks? If there is, delegate it to them and capitalize on the time that is now free. Utilize that to refocus your efforts on the most important tasks so your business can generate better revenues.

4. Switching from One Task to Another

Another hurdle entrepreneurs face when hoping to manage their time effectively is thinking that multitasking is beneficial and smart. They can't be more wrong as switching between tasks only keeps you distracted and unfocused. And any task completed without focus isn't going to cut—at least not in the longer run. So stop checking your email when working on an important worksheet as you might not like the price multitasking comes at.

Always try to get things done within a set timeframe. Once a task has been accomplished give yourself a 10-minute break and then start on the next one.

5. Traveling for Trips

If you are just building your startup from scratch, you might be tempted to travel to every happening seminar and conference. I won't lie, I was too! The temptation to be in the same room with your competitors, the other big names in the industry and to get a chance to introduce you and your brand to them is just every aspiring entrepreneur's dream. It took me some time to realize that the trips were unnecessary as most of the highlights from big workshops and seminars are placed on the internet a few days later. So if you come to think of it, you aren't missing out on a lot. Now imagine you spent that time elsewhere, such as building your brand, meeting new prospects, making important calls? Wouldn't that help your business better?

However, if you must travel, make the most of the time you spend traveling. Respond to any pending emails, declutter your inbox, make important phone calls, set up meetings for when you return, etc.

6. Being Unorganized

If you start your day without a to-do list, it becomes harder to focus your time and attention on things with the most promising outcomes and spend your time and efforts doing things that aren't that significant. Being organized prepares your mentality. You can achieve greater focus and concentrate your efforts on one task at a time. Have a to-do list prepared a day before for the following day so you prepare yourself to tackle that a day before. The more prepared you are, both mentally and physically, the better your chances of getting things done and dusted.

Managing time-wasters

To learn how to manage time-wasters, we first need to divide it into two categories. Time-wasters can either be external or self-general and internal. External time-wasters are things that other people such as your colleagues or clients may do to waste your time. Self-generated internal time-wasters, on the other hand, are things that you do that waste your time. Fortunately, self-generated time-wasters are much easier to control than external time-wasters.

Dealing with external time-wasters

Calls

Not all calls are important. Let your voicemail handle the non-urgent ones and allot time during the day to return those calls. Taking calls between tasks can trigger procrastination as well as lower your productivity levels. Chances are you will remain distracted for some time after the call, which means you just wasted time. And in business, lost time means lost dollars. When attending calls, be straight to the point so that the caller knows that you don't have the whole day to chit-chat. Keeping conversations short means you will have more time to schedule more important tasks.

Mail

Before you realize it, they fill every inch of your workstation. Sorting through your mail can be time-consuming and tedious. Therefore, to eliminate the waste of resourceful time, schedule a time in the day to go through it. Make it a practice to handle one mail at a time rather than just randomly opening each and addressing nothing. The more mail that pile up requesting an action, the more time you will end up throwing away.

Visitors

Visitors, whether they are colleagues, clients just dropping by to check on their projects or family or friends can eat up your time if you aren't aware. Keep your conversations small and stand when you feel like the conversation is becoming a drag. Standing up gives the impression that you are in a hurry to be somewhere and thus the visitor might cut short on their conversation. Moreover, you can move to your work station so that your back is toward the door. This makes one seem less approachable.

Dealing with self-generated time-wasters

Poor Planning and Lack of Priorities

A lot of entrepreneurs don't know where to start or how to proceed further on a commenced task. This results from a lack of planning. You must have a to-do list with you at all times so you can match your progress with your goals. You must also craft a list of priority tasks so that anything important is accomplished first. Keep a log of all your activities and notice if you are nearing your set goals or not. If not, they reprioritize and plan.

Procrastination

As stated in the first chapter, procrastination is your biggest enemy when trying to manage your time effectively. Always begin every task or project with a time of completion or deadline. Set rewards to serve as a motivator to keep you focused. Take breaks in between so that the task doesn't become too overwhelming. Try to work on it first thing in the morning so that you can concentrate better and complete it sooner.

Disorganization

If you are disorganized, chances are that you waste your valuable time looking and searching for things, sometimes on your desk, in your car or at your home. Try to organize things so that you can find them in time. Intend to have a clutter-free and clean work station so that you can remain focused on your task without getting up every few hours to look for a stapler, a punching machine or a document.

Habit 6: Living by the 80/20 Principle

An Italian economist in 1996, named Vilfredo Pareto once noticed how 20% of the pea pods in his garden produced 80% of the peas per year. This had him thinking if the same could be applied to economics as well? What if a small input can produce a larger economic output on a bigger scale? He tried to apply the concept in different industries, companies, and societies. His naïve hypothesis was true. 20% of the most productive faction produced 80% of the results.

Later, this came to be known as the Pareto Principle or the 80/20 principle. According to this principle, 80% of the output comes from 20% of the input or action. Meaning, if you focus all your energies on the 20% of one aspect, you can expect a return of 80%.

The 80/20 Principle became a popular subject in business management. Once applied, businesses were able to see that 20% of their customers did bring in 80% of the sales. They further found out that 20% of their sales representatives brought 80% of the sales and also that 20% of the costs led to 80% of the expenses.

When applied to time management, it was

revealed that 20% of the time yielded 80% of productivity and also that 20% of the employees created 80% of the value.

The Urgency for 80/20 Principle in the Life of an Entrepreneur

So if this were true, how can an entrepreneur use it to his/her benefit and manage time more efficiently? Let's take a look!

It is a common practice to note that small business owners or entrepreneurs just starting often waste their time on a $10 an hour job when they could easily be using the same amount of time on something with a $100 or $1000 per hour return. Forgoing activities with a better ROI for activities like running errands or performing routine tasks is looked down upon if you follow the principle. Instead of running around looking for the cheapest supplies, you could be spending the same time drafting important emails or negotiating more lucrative deals with potential clients.

Which sounds more beneficial in the long run?

But, alas, the problem remains the same. As entrepreneurs, we have the inborn tendency to manage everything on our own. We find it difficult to delegate tasks when we know we can do them. However, what we don't realize is the opportunity cost. Imagine you have a virus on your PC and you decide to look into it personally. You spend six hours trying to identify the problem and later end up calling a professional at last. There is no way you can bring back those six hours. The most you had to pay the computer guy is $10 or $20 per hour's work. If it took him less than an hour to fix the computer, that means that you not only wasted a good six hours but you also made no money when you technically should have made at least $60, were you an expert in fixing viruses.

Your job isn't to fix viruses but to bring in more clients, earn more revenue, deliver better products and services—a job that can easily pay you more than $60 per hour if you get into it.

You must understand that despite the urge to manage everything on your own, sometimes you have to look at the bigger picture and that is what the 80/20 principle is all about.

You want to be making the most of your time and ensuring that it isn't wasted on something as mediocre as a $10 job. Many businesses don't realize this until later and suffer at the hand of their foolishness.

How to Use the 80/20 Rule to Improve Productivity?

Now that I have you convinced that the 80/20 principle is what you must use to optimize your investments with the biggest chunk of money, the next step is learning how to use it to your advantage.

You have to agree that the 80/20 principle is a genius mindset in itself. It is even more remarkable when it comes to managing your time. It teaches you to let go of tasks such as fixing a leaky faucet, a virus, or personally answering to customer inquiries and outsource or delegate them so that you may spend the same time doing something far more productive and prolific for your business.

Evaluate and assess your tasks and goals

The first step to living by the 80/20 principle is assessing and evaluating your sets goals and objectives as well as what tasks you need to undertake to make them a reality. To help you decide what you should be doing instead of something else, ask yourself the following questions.

- Am I wasting too much time accomplishing specific tasks?
- Am I the most qualified individual for the task?
- Can someone else do it better and faster than you?
- Is this task as urgent as another one?
- Is this task going to take me one step closer to my goals?

Once you have this figured out, you need to move toward evaluating your goals once again. Are you investing your time in 20% with an 80% outcome or not?

Rework your to-do-lists

The next step is to rethink your to-do lists. Preferably, your to-do list should contain the top priority tasks. However, you must keep in mind that not every top priority task has the biggest outcome. True, your to-do list should be a reflection of your priorities but you must also acknowledge that not every priority task is worth making an effort for. If it is, then accomplish it first thing. If not, then you need to reassess your to-do list again, this time sequencing the tasks with the best use of time proportional to the most output.

Start with comparing each task with the effort required. Some tasks will require the most effort but have poor returns. Some tasks will require less time and effort but reap the most results. Which ones seem more appealing now that you have a new reevaluated to-do list listing all those tasks requiring minimum efforts but garnering the most results? They should now become a priority on your to-do list.

Ditch mediocre jobs

There are multiple menial tasks that you will stumble upon every day. The good thing about them is that you don't have to necessarily do them. You can always find someone else to do these. For instance, if you need some printer papers for your office, you can always send your assistant or driver to pick them up from the store. Or you could perhaps ask your secretary to clean up your inbox and desk. Delegating them not only ensures that the tasks will get done but also leaves you with free time to concentrate on something bigger and better.

Know when you work best

We all have a certain time of the day when creativity hits us. For some, it is early morning when the coffee kicks in, and for some it could be right after the lunch hour. Fathom at which time you are your most productive self. A time when you feel most energetic, enthusiastic, and mentally alert. Use that time of the day to schedule your most important tasks for the day. Attending to MITs during your prime time takes less time and effort compared to when trying to work on the same task when you are steamed out. And we just agreed earlier that prioritize tasks that take less time and effort and have greater returns, didn't we?

Take a break

A little break now and then can help clear your mind and allow you to focus better. A saturated mind is no good for you or your business. Pick up a good book, go to the park, eat out at your favorite restaurant, and spend some time with family and friends. Focusing too much on your work can leave you stressed as well as frustrated. Some downtime will surely relieve some of that stress and thus help you focus on the 20% with great concentration. Think about it, would you rather spend the whole day trying to accomplish the 20% or a few hours?

Eliminate interruptions

Distractions are around us all the time. It is up to us to either pay attention to them or not. They can come in the form of loud laughter in the copier room, in an email, as a social media notification, or a knock on the door. Distractions are unavoidable at times. You may not be able to avoid them entirely, but you can try to keep them at a minimum.

Make a list of the most common distractions during work hours. Notice how much time is wasted because of them. Once you have all of them listed, try to escape them by scheduling a certain time of the day to work on your 20%. For instance, if the majority of the interruptions are a result of notifications, messages, and calls on your phone, try to put it on silent before starting something important.

Chapter 4: Starting Your Day Early and Eating Healthy

In chapter 4, we shall be looking at how starting the day early boosts your productivity as well as allows you to better tackle the items on your to-do list. Secondly, we shall also learn about the importance of having a balanced diet. What foods are good for you and what you should be avoiding shall also be discussed in detail.

Habit 7: Starting Your Day Early

In many religions, starting your day early isn't just a lifestyle, but rather a requisite. The Buddhist monks wake up before the crack of dawn and get to their meditation, and the Muslims offer prayers early in the wee hours of the morning. The Hindus wake up early to pray to their respective gods. One of my great teachers once told me that how I start my day has a significant impact on how the rest of it will go. No research can prove that wrong! The wonders of starting your day early are numerous. First, it is the quietest time of the day which means zero distractions and interruptions. Secondly, the mind is refreshed early in the morning and has fewer things to think about, which means you also get mental clarity. Thirdly, as proven by research, our mind works at an optimum level 20 minutes upon waking up, which means you can rely on the ideas and creativity it comes up with.

The saying, "The early bird catches the worm" is very important to an entrepreneur. Not only does it warn you that to win over competition, you must start your day earlier, but it also tells you how to go about your day. Catches the worm means getting the right to work. Meaning, you don't just have to wake up early, you also have to start working right away. You must already know of many successful entrepreneurs and world leaders who wake up early. After all, when running the world, why would you want to miss a few hours of money-making for sleep?

We entrepreneurs are always on the lookout for that extra edge that would put our business on the way to commercial success. After all, this determination and relentless efforts are what differentiates us from average employees. We have a winning mindset, and we certainly won't settle for anything like mere survival.

One such difference can be trying to start earlier than the rest so that we can maximize the 24 hours at hand. The more time we waste, the less time we have left to work toward making our startup a success. It also slows our speed toward achieving our goals and ambitions.

Many entrepreneurs gloat of sleeping only a few hours in the day, but I won't recommend you any of that. As important as it is to work toward your goals, you also have to ensure your health. Comprising on your sleep isn't going to benefit you or your business. So try getting up early but getting in bed earlier. That should be the philosophy to live by.

All right, enough about getting up early. What

exactly does getting up early means? Is there a set time or hour that you need to get up at?

According to the new study published in the Wall Street Journal, 4 a.m. is the most ideal and productive time of the day (Potkewitz, 2016). The reasons are, of course, convincing such as minimal distractions, less activity on social media and no new emails or texts. And by productive, it doesn't only mean work-related productivity but productivity in general. And many had been following the regime of getting up at 4 a.m. long before the study was published.

- The CEO of Apple Inc., Tim Cook gets up as early as 3:45 a.m. and starts his day.
- The CEO of Virgin America, David Cush starts his day at 4:15 a.m. He listens to the radio, hits the gym, reads the paper and calls his associates on the East Coast to talk about business.
- The former president of Starbucks, Michelle Gass, starts her day at 4:30 a.m. sharp and goes jogging.

X Tips to Starting Early

Adapting a new timetable for waking up early is going to take some time. You can't expect yourself to go to sleep at 9 p.m. when you are conditioned to sleep at 11 p.m. Before you think about making such drastic changes, it is best to not overwhelm your brain and body. Instead of going to sleep at 9 p.m., try going to sleep at 10:30 p.m. Then gradually condition your brain to sleep a 10 p.m., then at 9:30 p.m. and then at 9 p.m. The same tactic applies to waking in the morning. Some other helpful strategies include:

Putting your Alarm Farther Away from the Bed

The biggest problems with alarms are that they are reachable. They come built-in our phones, which makes snoozing or disabling them a less-than-a-second chore. Have you ever wondered why is it so hard to go back to sleep once you have gotten up from the bed to close the window because the neighbor's dog is barking again or excess sunlight is penetrating the room? It's because you make a physical move from getting up from your bed. This tricks the mind into thinking it is time to get up.

Thus, if you have difficulty getting up early, set your alarm in a place away from the bed. You would have no other option to get up to disable it. Chances are, you won't want to fall back to sleep.

Turning on the Lights

If you plan to get up before the sun and stay up, turn on the lights into your room. Again, a hack to trick your brain into thinking it is daytime. Of course, you might want to snuggle up in bed for a few good minutes but not go back to a peaceful sleep.

Improving Sleep Quantity

For most people, getting a good seven to eight hours of sleep daily is a must. It seems like they are unable to function their best if they are sleep-deprived. If this is the case for you too, try getting in bed early so that you don't feel lethargic or fatigued upon waking up. You need that mind of yours to work its magic in an optimum manner.

Habit 8: Eating Right to Achieve the Highest Levels of Productivity

As an entrepreneur, your first goal is to ensure that your venture succeeds at all costs. When an entrepreneur starts, he/she will do all in their power to make it successful. I remember I used to work late, longer, and push myself constantly to up-level toward my set goals. I knew that if I worked harder then, I wouldn't have to work harder later. My goal was clear—I wanted to lead a carefree life when old. I wanted to earn a name for myself, have my startup recognized and save enough to never have to look at a price tag anymore. I searched the web for any inspirational stories, I looked up motivational speakers, and I read about the struggles of world-famous and successful entrepreneurs and leaders as I was determined to achieve it all before burning out.

What I didn't care for then was my health. The more hours I spent sitting down working toward my goals and chomping down junk food down my esophagus, the more weight I gained. I only realized it when I felt that it had started to hinder my ability to work, and I wasn't able to focus clearly.

When we neglect our health to put some more cash in the bank account, it can be detrimental in the long run. What will all that money be worth if you are no longer able to spend it doing the things you love? Building a successful career for yourself should indeed be the ultimate goal, but how will you if you aren't in good health? There have been cases of men having a heart attack in their mid-thirties due to pressure from work.

What if I tell you that eating healthy improves your ability to think better and be more productive? If that makes any sense, you can expect to make more money than before, don't you think? The more energized you are, the more productive you will be. The more productive you are, the more work you will get done. The more work you get done, the more money you will make. The formula is simple and has been in front of us all along. We just have been blind to see it. Eating right not only promotes good health but also improves our sleeping patterns, prevents us from becoming prone to self-inflicted diseases, and helps us achieve better clarity. Need more convincing? Check out some of the benefits of good nutrition and how it can help boost your mental health to keep your mind working at its full capacity.

How Good Nutrition Can Boost Productivity?

Like any entrepreneur, I am positive that you are crazed about getting more done in less time. To do just that, you make every second count and that means that they don't savor their food as most mindful practitioners do. They just gulp down whatever they can get their hands on. Now, I am not saying that all entrepreneurs are like that. I am just speaking on behalf of most of them.

Suppose you consume 2,200 calories per day. Our brain uses 20% of our total calorie intake for the day to function. In this case, this means it uses 450 calories. Since your brain is the powerhouse of all those amazing ideas, you must nourish it well. When you eat mindlessly and an imbalanced diet, you deprive your brain of glucose—that allows it to function optimally. Thus, you must nurture it with the right foods to promote a steady production and release of glucose so that your brain works efficiently and doesn't steam out.

And what happens when it works just fine? You can conquer the whole world. Your productivity improves, you take less time in developing ideas and roadmaps to your goals, you achieve mental clarity to put those ideas into practice and generate more revenue at the end of the day.

Another great thing that happens when you eat right is your stress levels decline. The never-ending fear of failure and making mistakes can make anyone sweat to the bone. And when a handsome amount of money and time are the parameters, you expect things to go smoothly. But even when everything goes smoothly, all ideas hit the mark, all opportunities are grasped at the right time, you still can't seem to calm yourself. Instead, the worry to move past these successes and onto the next one makes you anxious. And the day when stress starts to take over your mind, you are bound to make mistakes and make poor decisions—decisions that are shaped out of fear.

Luckily, the right foods can prevent that and lower the stress levels in your body.

Thirdly, it improves your brainpower. Like your body, your brain also needs fuel to process. Diets promoting healthy fats, raw fruits and vegetables, and lean meats have numerous benefits. One of those benefits is improved brainpower and memory. Moreover, it is pivotal that you keep in mind that it isn't just the food that you eat but also the foods that you don't eat, that makes the difference. If you can't eat healthily, you should try not to eat unhealthy either. Below are some of the things you should and shouldn't eat to keep your mind refreshed and your thought process clear.

- Eat foods high in Omega 3 content such as fish, nuts, and legumes.
- Limit your intake of calorie-ridden food such as butter, whole milk, cream, etc., as they impair memory and concentration.
- Consume more fruits and vegetables.
- Stay hydrated and drink more of fat-burning and energizing drinks such as herbal tea.

It also helps you make mental decisions faster as you have the clarity required to make sound decisions. Emerging science confirms that our diets play a crucial role in our cognitive functioning (Sarris, et al., 2015).

Eating the right foods offer better mental health where you can feel energized and pumped up. Moreover, another research study proposes that the fatter we get, the poorer our cognition. The studies were a result of decades of research and follow up studies where the participants who had gained weight showed mild impairments in their brain's functioning, memory, decision-making, and attention (O'Brien, Hinder, Callaghan, &

Feldman, 2017). Furthermore, the same study also revealed that people who consume more saturated fats than monounsaturated fats, they tend to have shorter recall and memory.

Eating healthy also prevents you from dying young. Death? Way to scare the lights out of you. It is true and frankly speaking, quite logical. Ask yourself, the day you started your business, what are the things you had to give up? Your sleep? Your free-time? Your carefree lifestyle and spending habits? And what did you gain in return? Constant anxiety, sleepless nights, skipping meals, and a never-ending fear of failure. How do all these affect you? They affect your health, digestive system, and metabolic rate. All these are classic precursors to developing heart diseases, cancer, diabetes, etc.

When you aren't eating right and out of shape, you pretty much risk developing any health condition known of. The poorer your eating habits, the likelier your decline in mental health and poor your energy levels. As an entrepreneur, you can't allow that.

Foods to Eat More Of

As stated above, a well-balanced diet consisting of good carbs, vitamins, proteins, and carbs will not only help you hone your cognitive ability but also offer your mental clarity as well as improved decision-making skills. When you feel energized, light-weighted and comfortable with your eating choices, you are bound to pay more attention to other important aspects of your business. You are also less likely to suffer from digestive and gastric issues which can be quite unpleasant to deal with. So what foods should you be having to improve your productivity and mental health? Take a look below at some of the most beneficial and productivity-enhancing food below.

- Eggs
- Yogurt
- Blueberries
- Walnuts and Almonds
- Bananas
- Spinach
- Avocados
- Eggplant
- Salmon
- Brown Rice
- Broccoli

Foods to Avoid

Some foods tend to promote sluggishness as well as sleepiness by making you feel fuller and bloated. When you don't feel comfortable in your skin, how do you propose to work at your full potential? Therefore, limiting them to a minimum will keep your health as well as the brain in check. Here are some foods that tend to offer temporary bouts of energy but leave you feeling bloated and lethargic.

- Coffee
- Sugary Drinks
- Calorie Ridden Fast foods
- Processed Meats

Chapter 5: Importance of Task Delegation and a Clutter-free Space

Not all tasks are for you to undertake. As an entrepreneur, your sole responsibility is to ensure that you continue progressing toward your goals and ambitions by working ONLY the most important tasks. An entrepreneur comes across many tasks that can easily be delegated to the staff under them. However, the decision to delegate is what most entrepreneurs find hard to address.

In habit # 10, we will be looking at how having a clutter-free space can make working less stressful, add to your focus and eliminate the unnecessary stationery and digital clutter that only adds weight. We look at different strategies on we can create a clutter-free space such as organizing the cables, digitalize the paperwork and moving the desk around.

Habit 9: Delegate Your Tasks to Save Time

Delegation is always a difficult task for entrepreneurs. They treat their startups like babies. It's hard to hand over their most beloved possession into the hands of someone else. Besides, they also think that no one, other than themselves can perform the tasks as they do.

But despite that delegation is a must for businessmen. After all, there is only a limited amount of things they can handle themselves. Delegation refers to the act of assigning responsibility and authority to someone with clearly-defined tasks to complete them successfully. In the business sense, it helps employees feel empowered and learn multiple traits from their boss.

In 2014, a survey from Gallup revealed that founders that had a team of dedicated high delegation talent had performed better than those without them (OTT & BADAL , 2015). Not only were they able to generate more business but also achieve success in them.

It isn't a requirement but a necessity in today's world. Delegation helps the business as well as the entrepreneur in two different ways.

First, it improves the efficiency of those given the tasks. Ideally, only those employees are awarded the responsibilities that the employer thinks can handle them best. Moreover, it leaves the employer with free time to capitalize elsewhere, in an area that is far more profiting. Besides, it doesn't make sense that the CEO of a company is doing administrative work, does it?

Secondly, the delegation also serves as a great idea to teach and coach employees that lack confidence in their capabilities to handle the additional task. It helps them to build and polish their skills and become confident at handling them.

The successful delegation includes the development of the right processes. There must be several expectations you will have from the individual taking over the task. You will seek feedback from others on how well or poorly they did. You will need to monitor their progress throughout the task completion. You will have to provide them with the resources required etc.

11 Tasks you Should Trust Your Employees With

So what tasks can and should you hand over to someone as competent as yourself? Take a look:

1. Administrative: Scheduling of appointments, managing calendars, booking airline tickets, sorting emails, returning phone calls on your behalf, etc. are all tasks that can easily be handed over to someone like an assistant so that you aren't distracted with these.

2. Accounting: Although you are entitled to keep track of your finances, hiring additional help to manage invoices, payrolls, record maintain or inputting financial info into ledgers can be extremely helpful.

3. IT Support: Got a virus on your PC? Are there any driver issues that need installations? Has the antivirus expired? All these are jobs that someone expert in IT support can handle with ease. Even if a step by step guide to fixing viruses is online, you don't have to waste an evening trying it out. Hire people who are experts at it and utilize that time doing something productive.

4. Routine Tasks: You are the entrepreneur for a reason. Your employees are your employees for a reason. There are tasks that

only you can perform and make you talented. However, anything that can easily be dictated and explained to an employee must be handled over. No need to keep yourself busy with things that undermine your true skills and abilities.

5. Website management: Of course, keeping an active presence online is essential for your business, but you don't have to type in all your content yourself on your website and social media accounts. Outsource it or hire people to do that. Writing requires research and typing—two of the most time-consuming things at times.

6. Marketing: As an entrepreneur, it is your job to devise and oversee your marketing strategy; however, you can always have a dedicated marketing team heading your brand's marketing, campaign designing, website copy, ad placements, etc.

7. Customer Support: As soon as your business takes off, you will be receiving plenty of calls and messages from customers offering feedback and complaints. An employee can take it up and report it to you later.

8. Banking: No one has the time to run to banks and collect every receipt of the purchases and transactions made. Even though most of it is digitized today, there's

nothing wrong with having a backup of receipts and important bank statements. Your job is to make money, let your employees handle the management.

9. Day-to-day inquires: Responding to everyday inquiries via emails or calls isn't what makes you a successful entrepreneur. Your brain, your performance strategies, your processes, and mindset is what makes you one. Even a shop owner can handle that.

10. Research: Even a kid of 10 knows how to Google (maybe just cartoons, but you get the point). You don't want to waste your valuable time to do basic research when someone can do it on your behalf.

11. Writing: Running a business no matter how big or small usually involves tons of writing and printing of reports, proposals, and blogs if you have an online website too. Despite being a good writer yourself, you don't want to waste your precious time typing into a computer when you can hire help. You can always edit the draft later and have it revised but don't start writing it.

Habit 10: Having a Clutter-free and Organized Space to Work

Many professionals think of a cluttered desk as something to be proud of. After all, doesn't that show how hard you work?

I strongly disagree as clutter just makes me disoriented for some reason. Every time I sense my desk becoming overcrowded or unorganized, it just puts me off. I have trouble finding things, little things frustrate me, and I certainly fail to concentrate on anything. If you feel like I am describing you, then good job, mate. You are one of those entrepreneurs who believe that a clutter-free space helps with improved productivity. I, for one, think that way.

A disorderly workstation isn't an inviting place to be. It can trigger a good amount of people and also gives the impression of you being careless and unconcerned about cleanliness. You don't want your employees to think of you that way. This calls for proper management of your desk, papers, and files as well as the furniture in your room.

Why it's time to Tidy Up?

If you think that your cluttered desk has no disadvantages, you would be surprised how much it can affect you and your productivity. And, oh, don't just take my word for it, I have scientific evidence that suggests it does affect your brain negativity and lead to procrastination.

It Triggers Stress

The very idea of a cluttered workspace is enough to trigger stress. You feel less motivated to work anywhere around it and become anxious when you have to look for an important document or piece of stationery from the messy workstation. Clutter also has the power to hinder our ability to work at 100%. A stressed mind isn't a product, and let's just leave it to that.

At Hampers with Creativity

Keeping a clean day is celebrated as a national day and for the very reason that a neat and clean workstation boosts productivity and keeps us inspired to work. I believe that the less clutter surrounds me, the more creative I am. I believe it happens for two reasons. First, I can focus my mind on singular tasks without worrying about the clutter and secondly, it keeps me distracted from what's more important.

It can be Distracting

Building more on the second reason above, it diverts the mind away from the actual task at hand. According to a study by researchers at the Princeton Neuroscience Institute, the more things that are in our view (sight) the increased chances of distraction (McMains & Kastner, 2011). How? Because all those things keep competing for our attention and most of the time we give in.

It Slows You Down

According to Entrepreneur, a survey found that the average worker can waste up to $4,800 just trying to find something (Matthews, 2014). Keeping your workspace clean will help improve your efficiency and help increase your company's productivity as a whole.

Clutter isn't only physical, it creates a vicious mental cycle that makes it hard to work efficiently and live a healthy active life.

Decluttering your Desk and Mind -Towards a More Productive You!

Now that we are aware of the many benefits of decluttering, it only makes sense that we get down to business and be done with it. Although, you can always hire external help, here's the thing. You will still need to monitor them so that nothing important goes down the bin, stolen or lost. So why not just start on your own?

Pick a time of the day when you are least busy. The time when there is rarely a knock on your door or messages on your phone, because you need to be clear-headed to start with. First, we shall look at how you can tidy up your desk and later how decluttering of the mind can be achieved as well.

Workspace Decluttering Tips

Physical clutter is always messier and harder to handle. It involves categorizing items, some labeling, some sorting and lastly, a handful of smart placement choices. As monotonous and unappealing as it may seem, it is a necessity. After all, we can't risk your brain going ineffective as soon as you enter your room or home office and look at all the clutter. Chances are any creativity that was breeding in your mind goes out the window. I recommend following a step-by-step approach to this.

Handle one task at a time

As stated up, the cleaning of the workspace doesn't just involve placing everything in the correct order. It also involves deciding what things need to stay, put away or go. This can be overwhelming for some. However, if you take one small step at a time, you might not find it difficult. Start with just one area or a drawer and reset it. When you tackle small tasks at a time and then excel at them, it serves as positive reinforcement. You feel like you have accomplished something and that kicker might just work for you to keep going. The idea is to get started and let the rest follow at its own time.

Reconsider Usage of Paper

In this adage of cloud-computing, why would you want to stack your desk with papers, after all? Minimize the usage and processing of paper. Besides, it is always a hassle to go through it all. On a computer, you can just search a certain work in the document and be directed to it in less than a second. Thus, anything that can be digitized, do it! Also, think about all those poor trees that sacrifice themselves just so you can have some paper to write on.

Deal with Your cables

Cables are unmanageable. They get tangled, get stretched, and create a spark and what not. The worst thing—they can't be avoided. Although smartphone companies are investing in some good model charging devices without cables, desktop, laptops, and tablets still have a long way to go. If you happen to have all these in your work station, I can easily assume your frustration. Fortunately, there are some inexpensive cable boxes and power cords you can buy and keep them in place and away from your desk. Furthermore, make it a habit to put them away in a drawer or in a cabinet when not in use to maximize the free space on your workstation.

Mind Decluttering Tips

A lot of people think that there is no such thing as mental clutter, but they couldn't be more wrong. Mental clutter is far worse than workspace clutter, as it leaves you helpless at most. Unlike digital or desk clutter, you can't see or touch it, which makes the cleaning process even harder. A cluttered mind is full of ideas as well as distracting thoughts. It makes focusing trickier and you may find yourself being unable to process your thoughts or complete tasks. If you have a cluttered mind, chances are that you have many pending tasks that you wanted to finish but couldn't as something always distracted you. If this is the case, it isn't a good one. Luckily, there are ways you can manage the clutter and keep it from lowering your levels of concentration.

Make to-do lists

Has it ever happened to you that you are trying your best at completing a task but something keeps popping into your head? Perhaps a better idea for another project, a new way of doing things, or new marketing means? If yes, then the best way to take them out of your head is to put them on paper in the form of a to-do list. Having a list also keeps you on your toes and busy, as you don't want the items on the list to keep piling up. A to-do list also happens to improve your memory as anything written down is hard to miss when the time comes to work onto them.

Journalize Your Thoughts

Writing down your ideas and thoughts puts them onto paper—a place other than your head. Once you have them journalized, they will stop bothering or distracting you. Moreover, you can use the journal like your to-do list as well and scribble down all your goals, visions, and plans on how you are going to work toward them and accomplish them.

Chapter 6: Task Prioritization and Scheduling

In this chapter, we shall learn about the importance of task prioritizing with the help of some renowned and well-tested theories such as the ABCDE method, Eating the Frog, Eisenhower Matrix, etc.

Later, in habit 12, we discuss how important scheduling tasks are in a planner or calendar and how to create a to-do list that involves all the most important tasks in a prioritized order.

Habit 11: Prioritizing Tasks

We have already looked at numerous strategies for singling out a task and making it a priority, but I believe there is so much to offer in this regard that you just can't seem to leave it behind.

Task prioritization is a must for entrepreneurs with big dreams and goals. It allows us to manage our time more efficiently and also be able to say "I did that" at the end of the day. Task prioritization is also important because aspiring entrepreneurs often waste their time doing things that can easily be delegated, postponed to another date, or simply eliminated. Yes, there are so many redundancies that we fail to acknowledge and eventually end up doing them.

Although we have discussed all of this earlier as well, we haven't looked at task prioritization from and urgency or an important aspect. When in a fix with multiple important to-dos on your list, how to go about picking the one that should be completed first thing? See, there is where the dilemma lies. You may have a list of important tasks on hand but do you know in which order are you going to accomplish them?

It all starts with creating a to-do list of all the tasks you wish to achieve. If you don't have an overview of all the things you wish to achieve, then how would you prioritize any? Take the time out to write down all the tasks for the day so that you are clear on what you wish to achieve by the end of this working day.

Once you have all the tasks listed down, set a time frame for each of the tasks. Also, circle out the top three that you wish to achieve at all costs before the day ends. This will leave you with three such tasks that must be accomplished no matter what. What you did there was adding a sense of urgency and importance to them. However, we are still not done as you still need to figure out which one to take on first.

Below are some great full-proof techniques by some of the most successful entrepreneurs and business leaders to help you sort.

The How-To aka Techniques that Work

ABCDE Method

The ABCDE method helps with the identification of which task holds the most important and set it as your top priority. It helps differentiate between two tasks that seem equally important. Developed by Brian Tracy, it will help you categorize your tasks on not one but multiple levels of importance. Here's how you can use it to your advantage.

If you have more than one important tasks listed on your to-do list, thoroughly go through it and give each task an alphabet from A to E. Task with A written in front of it ranks highest on your priority and vice versa. For tasks with A in front of them, add a number to them starting from 1 (1 being highest on your list of priority)

Do the same for all the tasks listed B, C, D, and E. Each task should have an alphabet and a number. Here's what each alphabet stands for.

- A: Very important, can't be ignored, negative consequences attached if not completed.
- B: Important but less important than task A, minor negative consequences.
- C: Tasks that are nice to do but not as important as A or B, no negative consequences attached if you don't complete them.
- D: Tasks that should and can be delegated to save time and work on tasks A and B instead.
- E: Tasks that can be eliminated or left behind to free up some time for tasks A and B

Warren Buffet's Two-List Strategy

If you are working toward the wrong goals, there is no point in being efficient. Therefore, it is important that you keep reassessing your goals from time to time to evaluate your long-term goals so that you don't end up regretting over some missed opportunity, says Warren Buffet, the world's biggest investor.

According to Mr. Buffet, you must start with a list of 25 goals you want to achieve. They can be anything such as leading global business to learning how to cook. The goals can be related to your career, your personal life, or even your hobbies such as learning to play piano professionally.

Next, circle five goals you want to accomplish no matter what. The goals that, according to you, are the most important in your life.

Now, look at the remaining 20 goals that you didn't draw a circle onto. These are goals that you must AVOID AT ALL COSTS. Yes, you heard that right. You have to forget about accomplishing them altogether because, in your mind, they take a low position. Meaning, your hearts not entirely into accomplishing them and you wouldn't have any regrets if you didn't accomplish them ever.

The five circled goals should now be your new to-do list and you must only work toward ensuring that you accomplish them at all costs. Way to go, Mr. Buffet.

Ivy Lee Method

Sometimes, despite having a dedicated to-do list on our calendars, we still end up with more than what we can handle on our plates. There can be more than one important task that you wish to achieve. So, how can you further dig through them to prioritize them in order?

Use the Ivy Lee Method.

The Ivy Lee method is a 100-year-old strategy that still gets the best of the world's best entrepreneurs. It has paved the way for some of the most brilliant business and time management strategies. It was designed by a productivity consultant called Ivy Lee, thus the name. Here's how you can use it to shortlist which tasks should be prioritized first and why.

At the end of your day, before going to bed, make a list of the six most important tasks that you want to accomplish the next day. Prioritize those in an order you wish to perform them based on their importance. When the next day begins, focus solely on the first task and don't move onto the second until you have finished the first one. Go through the other items on the list similarly until you are done with all the tasks on your to-do list. Then after this day, make another list of six of the most important tasks and finish them in the same manner.

Eat the Frog

Please don't mistake it for a literal suggestion as this is just another method to prioritize your tasks. It is inspired by the famous quote by Mark Twain, "If it's your job to eat a frog, it's best to do it first thing in the morning." In the world of business, it translates into accomplishing the biggest or most challenging tasks first thing in the morning. Tasks that are top-priority and promise the greater good should be the ones you should tackle first. Once you are done eating the frog, aka accomplishing the most important task for the day, you can divide your time into working on the less important ones throughout the day.

For instance, if you have a big meeting planned for the coming Monday, instead of wasting your time organizing your email folder or doing other menial tasks, devise a plan on how you are going to deliver your point of view in the meeting such as what points will be discussed, what response would you have for any backlash, how you are going to handle the question and answer session, etc. You can always go back to organizing your inbox once you are prepared for the big meeting.

Eisenhower Matrix

The Eisenhower Matrix is another famous and workable tool to help you set your priorities straight.

It is divided into four matrixes or quadrants, into a four-square grid. The top column quadrants are labeled as Urgent and Not Urgent, whereas the top two rows are labeled Important and Not Important. It helps the user decide which task to place in which quadrant based on how urgent or important it is. It is known to expedite time management. You start by listing all your day's tasks into different boxes sorted by priority. Once you have them placed, start with tasks that lay in the Urgent and Most Important quadrant and complete the first and dismiss the ones that find a spot in Not Urgent/Not important quadrant.

Below is a representation of what each quadrant represents.

- Urgent/Most Important (tasks you MUST DO instantaneously).
- Important/Not urgent (tasks you want to

schedule for later).
- Urgent/Not important (tasks you can and should delegate).
- Neither urgent/Important (tasks that can eliminate).

Habit 12: Schedule Your To-Dos Religiously

An entrepreneur is no less than a martyr, especially those just starting. They rarely have any time to shut the eye, are taking up all orders as they come in, making big promises, adding more and more tasks in their to-do lists and taking every bad feedback on their shoulders for the sake of survival and the cruel and competitive business world.

Generally, the obsession with to-do lists is understandable. It boosts productivity and keeps you motivated and clear-headed. Multitasking, on the other hand, is seen as downright destructive as it leaves one confused and mingled in between multiple tasks nowhere near their completion. Despite that, entrepreneurs keep piling more projects and tasks that they can take upon and just adding more stress. You won't get any bonus hours in the day because you have your plate too full. So why exhaust yourself in trying to achieve everything at once by putting too many tasks on the to-do list?

One of the biggest risks with overpromising is failing to live by them. Thus, to become a successful business owner, strive for more free space on your list rather than overcrowding it.

Why Schedule?

Scheduling your to-do list is constructive for several reasons. For starters, it brings you closer to your goals and ambitions as you just work upon the things that will eventually take you there. Furthermore:

- It allows you to create a mental note of all the things you can achieve in a given amount of time REALISTICALLY.
- It ensures that you give each task the desired time it needs.
- You are left with some contingency time in case something goes wrong.
- It helps you achieve that work-life balance you crave so much.
- It allows you to only take on as much as you can handle and eliminate all such tasks with little value.

As entrepreneurs, we need to understand that the time we waste on doing something unproductive or of little value, it's never going to come back. It isn't like a missed opportunity that will find a way back to you at some point in your life. Once it is gone, there is no coming back and regret should be the least of your worries when building an enterprise. Scheduling isn't just a day's activity, you need to be clear about what you want to achieve today, tomorrow, a week from now, months later and after a year or so. When you do it in this manner, you create a pathway for yourself to follow through and make your dreams a reality.

The Requisites of Scheduling

Thanks to the internet-powered world, we now have a bunch of great apps to schedule our to-do lists, I still prefer the pen and paper method over it. It just gives me such pride cutting out the tasks after they are completed. The satisfaction is incomparable, to be honest. However, if you find online planners more convenient, I don't have any problems. The important thing is to have everything scheduled and organized so that you can start right away without wasting any time.

Follow the steps below to create one from scratch and get working.

Detect Available Time

The first step is to identify how much time you are willing to work in the day. Entrepreneurs who are just starting tend to spend more time working as they have to set their brand. Once that is achieved, the working hours can be minimized. Establish how many hours you are going to be working so that you can see how many tasks you can fit in the day.

Schedule Important Actions

The second step is to find out what actions are required to take the task to completion. For instance, if you wish to conduct a mentor session for your employees, ensure that the meeting room is set, your presentation is prepared and your employees have been notified about the session before its beginning.

Plan Top-Priority Tasks

The next important step is to list and review all those top-priority tasks and maintenance tasks that you need to complete and no one other than you can do. Make sure that you organize the tasks for a time of day you are your most productive. For instance, if your creativity kicks in first thing in the morning or right after the lunch break, schedule the most important tasks at that hour so that you can maximize focus.

Keep Free Time in Between Tasks

It is praiseworthy that moves from one task onto another right away so that you can be done on time. However, it isn't ideal. Sometimes, some tasks take more time than anticipated and thus put you behind on your schedule. Therefore, when planning tasks, have a 15-30 minutes free time in between each task. Even if everything goes smoothly, you can use that time to refresh your mind with something other than work-related. This time is also for coping with any contingencies such as another important thing coming up.

Chapter 7: Looking Past Failures and Achieving Focus with Single Tasks

A lot of times, entrepreneurs have a tough time dealing with failures and missed opportunities. In this chapter, we shall look at what can be done in this regard and learn of full-proof tips that can help overcome the stress and regret associated with it.

Later we move on to discover the benefits of working at a single task at a time and the benefits single-tasking holds over multitasking.

Habit 13: Stopping to Regret Over Failures and Mistakes

Research shows that out of every 10 startups three or four are bound to fail miserably. Of the remaining, three to four make it past their initial investment, whereas only one or two provide the owners with substantial returns (Gage, 2012). To put it more precisely, 95% of startups fail.

All entrepreneurs know that running a new venture is no funny business. It's gambling right there with no upper hand whatsoever. There are complicated decisions that one must take such as which opportunities are worth investing and which must be let go. No matter how hard you try, there will be times when your carefully laid-out plans will fall flat. It can be investing in the wrong opportunity or not investing in the right one. It could be lacking a long-term vision. It could be focusing too much on earning money rather than a name.

The case being, we have, at some point failed at our attempts and suffered due to bad advice or implementation. But what is next? Is there no way to see past that? Do you decide to pack up after the mistake right away?

No, you don't. Instead of crying over them, you

need to move on and take the next train. The next opportunity could be just past the door. Are you not tempted to open the door and see what it is?

How to Move Past Entrepreneurial Failure?

Anyone who has lost big is bound to have a tough time in life. But you will be surprised that even the best and biggest of brands made the worst advertising blunder and are still in business, so how can one small mistake make you want to quit?

In 1985, during a blind taste test, people were asked to choose which cola they like the best— Coke or Pepsi. The cola wars were in its prime and both the companies were trying to establish themselves as the most liked. When most of the participants preferred the taste of Pepsi over Coke, this had the company scratching their heads for new ideas. They hastily came up with a new drink called the "New Coke." They redid the 100-year-old formula all over and added more sweetness to their drinks. They boldly launched it in April 1985 without realizing that the data had been wrong. True, the people had admired the taste of Pepsi in a blind taste test but only for the first sip. They unanimously agreed that Coke was much better and slightly less sweet in comparison with Pepsi, making it more likable when drinking a can. So the decision to add more sweetness backfired badly, and Coke had to admit that it was a disaster.

Another classic example comes from Hoover, a household name in the vacuuming industry, primarily in the UK. You wouldn't ever think that the company would make such a crummy math blunder that generations would learn from forever. The company suffered from a backlog of aging vacuums and wished to sell immediately. So someone in the company thought of a deal that was too good to be refused. The deal was beyond stupidity. Two free plane tickets to the U.S. for anyone who purchases more than £100 in their products. The company thought that in such high rates of inflation, only a few would be able to avail the offer, but to their surprise, 222,000 people purchased products worth £100 and earned a roundtrip to the U.S. Due to high inflation rates, each customer received $1,500 in airfare. The company's net worth went from £50 million to $68 million to become bankrupt.

So if they can move past that, why can't you? Below is a full-proof strategy to help you get over your failures and prepare yourself for what's next to come. Who knows you could be the next biggest cola drink manufacturer—minus the blunder?

Own up to it

The first step to moving past your failures and mistakes is to accept that you made one. If you won't acknowledge it, you will keep going back and forth mapping all the aspects of it, wasting time over something that can't be undone. You don't want to be carrying dead weight on your shoulder. You must recognize that your plan didn't work, and the opportunity had been missed. Once you are past that, you can move onto the next step which involves letting go.

Move on

A wise princess once said, "Let it go" and she wasn't wrong. There is no point looking back and wishing you could have done things differently. Perhaps, it wasn't a failure on your part but someone else's. For how long will you keep regretting over it. Did you know nobody wanted to hire Albert Einstein as a professor once? JK Rowling didn't have her books published by the first publisher she sent her drafts too. There were innumerable publication houses that rejected her work. The point being, losing is one chapter in your book of life, not the whole book. If you keep thinking about past failures, you will never be able to move forward with new ideas and doubt your abilities.

Learn

As important as moving on is, learning why it happened is also imperative. After all, wouldn't it be insanity if you make the same blunder again? Therefore, you need to know where things went wrong so that you can do better the next time around. You need to ask yourself those hard questions and accept the answers with an open mind.

Look for the positives

There is always a silver lining. Okay, that sounded poetic but it is true. Even the worst of failures leave behind something. Sometimes it is a positive message that can change your mindset and working style completely. It could also mean looking at the mistake from a different angle and learn what it could mean. Is there anything good to learn from it? Perhaps, you moved too fast. You could slow down and give all your decisions a second thought. Perhaps you were too focused on the results when you should have been focused on the task. You could try that the next time. There is always something you can learn from failure and mistake.

Habit 14: Achieving Focus with Singular Tasks

If I leave with you a quote by Stephen R. Covey, I think there will be nothing left for me to say or emphasize onto. Nonetheless, I am going to and I am also going to share with you the quote.

"The main thing is to keep the main thing the main thing."

There, was I wrong? The quote in itself is a whole book just waiting to be written by someone as passionate as myself about the importance of single-tasking. The opposite of multitasking, single-tasking focuses on building a laser-sharp focus on just one task at a time.

James Clear, another writer specializing in self-improvement says, "Focus can only occur when we have said yes to one option and no to all other options."

Single-tasking –It's an Art too!

The majority of entrepreneurs like to have all of their plates spinning at the right time. Think of them as a magician trying to pull off multiple tricks at the same time. Not only does it make it harder to perform one with full concentration, but it also leaves the audience baffled as to what is happening. As the wise men say, too much of anything is dangerous. As moguls, we always think about the big picture. Don't get me wrong— there isn't anything wrong with focusing on the big picture, it is just that, doing things hastily and all at once is a fail-strategy. And I will tell you why.

Multitasking keeps one preoccupied with the things they aren't even doing but had been doing just a while ago, taking away all the focus and concentration from what they are doing right now. The attention keeps drifting from one thing to another and then onto the next one, making focusing on just one almost impossible. Sometimes, the distraction comes in the form of a text, an email, a phone call or a picture of your favorite celebrity on the internet. The mental haze blinds us. The goal was to achieve more in less time but the result is completely the opposite. Nothing gets done on time and stresses you out further.

With single-tasking, you can sustain focus even when working on something complex.

Single-tasking enables you to sustain your focus and work through complex problems. It also reduces your level of stress about numerous other things. Here's a fact. The more you try to do at once, the more boggled and confused your mind becomes until there comes a point when it completely shuts down. When you multitask and fail to achieve any measurable success, you spend more time trying to fix where you went wrong and thus further slow down on your goals and tasks. In retrospect, when you focus on just a single task at a time, you can tap into the most unknown areas of your brain and bring out some of the best ideas you never thought would come from your mind.

Next, the management of work becomes easier. With just one task scheduled for a fixed period, you don't have to go back and forth, wasting time on trying to achieve it all. Single-tasking also helps you identify the most important tasks and how you can make your time most productive.

Finally, the sense of completion and achievement is one of the greatest feelings in the world. Thankfully, with single-tasking, this doesn't only remain a dream. The feeling is motivating as well as satisfying. Even if you just undertake a single task in the entire day instead of several, you will still have something to show and feel proud of at the end of the day. This satisfaction is rare with multitasking, as many tasks are half done and you are left with nothing progressive to show or be proud of.

Taking One Task at a Time –How-To

Single-tasking prevents one from switching between tasks but rather focuses all their strength, mental capability, resources and time in a single task. But that sounds too good to be true, right? It doesn't ONLY sound good in theory but in practice too. Here's how you can learn to put in all your focus on a single task without becoming distracted by the other pending tasks or the things around you.

Block the Ringing

Imagine you are too engrossed in a task and near completion. The next second, your phone vibrates and you check it to find a message from your wife that you need to pick up her car from the auto repair. And then another one is followed by that statement that you need to bring along some things from the grocery shop as well.

What follows next is you waiting impatiently for that list to come through and later plan your route in that manner. Your mind immediately shifts from the task and onto planning your returning route and time.

What did that one message do? It takes your attention away from the actual and far more important task and onto something that could have easily waited until you were done with it.

Notifications like these can disrupt the rhythm of your work, and it is easy to lose concentration. Thus, if possible, when trying to focus your attention on a single task, have your phone on silent or away from your reach so you aren't tempted to go back and check for new messages or notifications.

Allocate Time Strategically

To optimize focusing on a singular task, you must set a time limit to complete it. If you can divide the tasks into multiple smaller tasks and working on each step one at a time, then allocate time for each task to be completed. The fear of falling behind will keep you on your toes and your mind focused, helping you successfully finish it.

Take Breaks

A singular task is bound to become monotonous after some time. After all, we all don't have the attention span of a lion eyeing its prey or a crocodile planning its next move. We are likely to feel bored and lose focus. Thus, refreshing your mind from time to time is another requisite you must indulge yourself into. There comes a point, when after some time, the brain becomes numb to the stimuli, making the task less interesting. Taking small breaks in between can help your brain refocus better as it gets recharged.

Chapter 8: Scheduling Time for Tasks and Building a Goals vs. Dreams List

In this chapter, we walk across two habits revolving around the importance of task scheduling and building a list of achievable goals. Along the way, we learn how scheduling tasks ahead of time can enhance productivity and improve mental clarity and how having a goal-oriented to-do list can take us closer to achieving our goals.

Habit 15: Stop Overspending Time to Complete Tasks

Do you always find yourself complaining about a lack of time on your hands? Do you always find yourself working until the very last minute before the deadline and wonder how did it take you so long to get done with it?

When I first started writing this book, I told myself that I would have it finished by the end of the month. Everything was on the tips of my fingers, I just had to sit down each day for a specific amount of time and start writing. However, no such thing happened and by the end of the month, I didn't even have a rough draft to show as my accomplishment. It may sound strange coming from someone who boasts of effectively managing time but let me tell you, sometimes it even gets the best of us.

Now that I look back, I was wrong in two aspects. First, I had a defined deadline, i.e. the end of the month, but I didn't have one for daily. I knew I had to write every day but how much and for how long it wasn't clear. Therefore, there were days when I barely got some 500 words scripted and days where I couldn't stop writing even after 5000 of them.

When I realized that and set a time frame for each day, I made the second blunder. I overestimated the time. I gave myself too much of it and ended up accomplishing very little. That, my friends, is the bigger problem—not knowing how much time each task requires and if you are just overspending it. Even when I had plenty of time to reach the daily word-limit, I failed to do so. I was always distracted by other things, thinking, "Hey, I still have an hour to write. How about I watch some sports before going back to writing?"

So the problem wasn't that the task was too hard but that I had given myself too much time to finish it.

Ideally, any task, big or small, should be allotted 20 to 60 minutes to complete. Do you know that working more hours has nothing to do with progress? There is no award for someone who completes a task in two hours if the task only required one.

Spending too much time on a single task also affects your overall productivity. In an age where entrepreneurs have a jam-packed list of tasks, wasting too much time on just one or two means most of them will remain unfinished by the end of the day. Ask yourself does that sound like a productive day to you?

We often believe that when we spend too much time on something, it is our best work. But go back to the time when you were in college and partied hard until the last week or night before the exams. Did you not pass? Maybe not with the grades you had hoped for, but you still got through and look where you are today. This means that spending too much time doing one thing doesn't necessarily mean that it was required. Some people work best under pressure and in stressful work conditions because that is when they believe they are their most productive.

So how to determine how much time do you need for a single task and how to train your brain into accomplishing it in the given timeframe? It is difficult, but doable. Take a look below for some great tips for help.

The Only Guide You Need For Correct Time Allocation

Start with an expected Outcome

One of the primary reasons the majority of us spend too much time on a particular task is because we are unfamiliar with what to expect. Unless you know what will be the outcome and in what ways is it going to benefit you, how can you allocate time to it? This leads to wasting time on things that aren't as necessary as the others. So the first step to time allocation is determining what tasks deserve our time and efforts and reimbursements they will offer.

Create an Appointment

Or a completion date on your to-do list and calendar so you know the extent of time that has been awarded to you. A deadline will help you remain focused as well as serve as a motivator to keep you going. That way, you won't waste time on something redundant and save time.

Begin with Singular Tasks

Working on a singular task promotes the completion of it. After all, when you have 10 items in your to-do list and you are only on the first one, you keep track of every minute that has been spent and keep monitoring how much time you further need and how much will be left for the other tasks.

Stop when Done

Well, that sounds logical but rarely practiced. A lot of times, when we are done with a task in less time than allotted, we keep going back to polish it further and waste valuable time, which can be utilized elsewhere. Imagine if the additions add no value to what you had already accomplished. How would that feel? Therefore, the moment you think you are done with something, move on to the next task.

Habit 16: Build a Goal vs. Dream List

What are dreams if not accomplished? Wise men call goals as dreams with a time limit. Dreams are the visions you set for your company, the ambitions you have and your desires to take it to the top. Goals, on the other hand, are the actionable steps you need to take to get there. They are steps that turn your dreams into reality.

Below are some of the biggest differences between the two.

- Dreams are ideas you can only think about, whereas goals are ideas you can work upon.
- Dreams don't have an expiration date or a deadline but goals usually do. You can dream forever, but you must put a date on achieving your goals.
- Dreams don't produce any beneficial results unless worked upon. Goals produce results—sometimes good and sometimes bad.
- Dreams are free of any monetary implications, whereas you have to pay a price to achieve goals. It can be tangible as well as intangible.
- Where dreams are often imaginary, goals

are a reality. You can dream of growing wings and flying high, but that is unlikely to happen. Alternatively, goals are things you can accomplish in real life.

- Dreams are inspirations that keep you motivated. Goals have the potential to change your life.
- You don't have to stop dreaming ever, but with goals, there usually is an ending point.
- Dreams don't have a focus and can be abstract, unlike goals. Goals require focus and determination, otherwise the outcome won't be a desired one.
- Dreams don't require any work but rather just some imagination. The accomplishment of goals requires work—sometimes endless hours, weeks, months or years.

Unlike, goals, dreams can sometimes be unrealistic. There is only an extent to what we can do. Dreams aren't measurable whereas goals are. Therefore, to set realistic and achievable goals, it is important to create a to-do list that promises prosperity as well as monetary benefits.

So what should you go after? Goals or Your Dreams

Now that we realize what results in actual success, it only makes sense to create a to-do list based on actual and accomplishable goals. If you have something such as wanting to be Superman on your list, it isn't something achievable. You can definitely hope for some miracle.

So your emphasis should be only building a list of tasks revolving around your goals. There is a universally-accepted strategy to create a goal-oriented to-do list, called the SMART strategy. Take a look at what it represents.

SMART stands for:

- Specific
- Measurable
- Achievable
- Realistic
- Timely

Let's see what each of these individually embody and how does it help you create a brilliant to-do list.

Specific

Goals that have been specified or come tied to

some consequences have a greater chance at completion. But how do you know a goal is specific? Moreover, what if you have more than one goal? Ask yourself the following questions to determine an order at which each should be accomplished.

- What benefits does it promise?
- Why do I want to accomplish it?
- Is it worth the effort and time spent?
- Who will benefit the most from it?
- How soon do I want to achieve this goal?

Suppose you are confused between two goals—earning profits and brand awareness. Ask yourself the questions above to determine what equals more benefits in the long run and then use that goal as your 'specific' goal.

Measurable

The goal's success or failure should be measurable to help you decide whether it's worth the undertaking. Thus, establish measurable criteria to determine its importance and worth.

Achievable

Next, the goals have to be achievable, as stated above several times. Goals that are challenging yet doable makes one want to achieve them.

There is a sense of motivation and responsibility associated with it.

Realistic

A goal should be achievable in the set time frame. You must be able to finish it with measurable efforts and resources.

Timely

Lastly, the goals should be time-bound so that its completion becomes a reality and compulsion. Not setting a date to accomplish the goal will only lead to procrastination till the very last minute, which isn't something you want.

Chapter 9: Importance of a Stress-free Environment and Disconnecting from Social Media

Ever wondered how crucial the working conditions are and how they affect your work? As entrepreneurs, we each have a different way of handling things. Some of us work best under pressure, whereas others prosper better when they work in a time constraint environment. Despite our differences, we must understand that the work environment can have a significant impact on your productivity. The more productive we are, the more work we shall get done in a timely fashion.

One of the reasons we fail to work our best is because we are surrounded by distractions from all corners. The biggest source is social media. It wouldn't be wrong to say that we are addicted to our devices. We are always scrolling through multiple social media channels or following the latest trends set by our favorite celebrities. What we fail to see is the impact it has on our work.

In this chapter, we are going to be addressing

both of these habits and help you understand why you need to limit your time on social media as well as create a stress-free working environment.

Habit 17: Creating a Stress-Free Work Environment

Several different work environments can be quantified and measured. A stress-free workspace means that one feels anything but stressed when in that space. A working condition is bound to arouse some sort of feeling such as happiness, anger, or anxiety. Perhaps, it is the colors on the walls that keep distracting you or little cubicles that leave you with no privacy. It also refers to the relationship between the employee and employer and the communication between them. The more stringent the relationship, the more pressured and stressed your employees will feel.

A stress-free environment improves your morale and productivity. When there is good communication among the employees and employers, there will be a little delay in the work and thus enhanced productivity.

When you create a stress-free environment for yourself and your employees, you eliminate the chances of distractions that result in stress. As a result, deadlines are met and everyone performs better than they should. Your job as an entrepreneur is to ensure that the stressors are identified before they begin to hinder the work.

When that happens, the management of projects becomes smoother and everyone feels motivated to give their 100%.

How to Create a Stress-Free Environment to Boost Productivity

Identify the Stressors

As stated earlier, the first step involves the identification of what causes stress. Sometimes the stress stems from the guilt of not being able to give time to your family or friends. Other times, it is the pressure of a new project, an approaching deadline, difficulty with clients, negative feedback from customers, etc., thus as soon as you identify one, nip it in the bud by addressing it instantaneously.

Change up your routine

Routines can become monotonous and boring. Like any relationship requires some spicing up, so does your routine. Sticking to the same routine can also breed procrastination and lower your level of focus. This can also be one of the reasons for stress. Make small but significant changes in your work routine so that you feel less stressed going in for work every day. Make time for a few hobbies and interests between each task so that you don't feel bored or zoned out.

Share the load

Excessive workload is another reason for stress. Delegation of some tasks can help build a better and more confident entrepreneur. When your mind is occupied with too much, it takes more time to work through things as the constant stress keeps slowing things down. It will also drain out sooner than expected because the large amount of work seems non-accomplishable. Therefore, whenever possible lower the load on your shoulders and share it with others.

Habit 18: Disconnecting from Social Media Bombardment

Social media indulgence is becoming a nuisance for everyone. There is so much happening to everyone that you just don't want to miss out on anything. This leads to an unhealthy addiction and obsession with our gadgets, which hinders the competition of tasks as well as declined productive and attention.

As a thriving entrepreneur, the majority of your time should be emerged in running a successful venture. Anything else should come second. If it doesn't then that, right there, is a problem you need to address. It isn't wrong to say that social media has taken over our lives. Despite being a means of communication, it is distancing us from the things we previously enjoyed or spent time doing.

The Harmful Implications of Social Media Indulgence

In 2015, a research study conducted by the Pew Research Centre revealed that the more engaged we are in the online world, the more stressed we are (Hampton, Rainie, Lu, Shin, & Purcell, 2015). The stress comes breeds from the fact that whenever we go online, we come across someone else's life that seems more interesting than ours. This triggers the feelings of stress and loneliness as well as unhappiness. As an entrepreneur, seeing your competition succeed can leave you feeling like a failure and induce stress and anxiety.

Social media can also promote feelings of hopelessness and insectaries affecting our focus and long-term goals. The less confident we are of our strategies and work processes, the higher at risk we are of leaving them half-done. When we start believing that we won't get where we want to be just because someone else didn't, it depresses us.

In conclusion, people who are heavy users of social sites also report poor mental health. This can easily affect your mood and make you angry or frustrated. The more time we spent together, the more social comparisons we make with other's lives. And as the saying goes, the grass is greener on the other side, we often end up comparing our lives with people who have it all.

How to Limit Social Media Addiction?

Set boundaries

Overindulgence of anything is harmful and this is accurate for the bombardment that social media is in our lives. Identify why you are so obsessed with it and what makes you go back online every few hours. Is it the nearness of your phone, some tedious task or just too much free time on your hands? Set daily parameters so that you spend only a limited amount of time online. If the monotony of the task is the issue, address it with finding ways to make the task interesting and fun. If too much free time is the problem, then you need to reassess your to-do list and add a few more tasks for the day so that you remain preoccupied. If the nearness of your phone is the real culprit, set it aside and on silent so that every time you think about opening Facebook, you have to make the effort to get up and get it. Chances are, you won't do it often.

Set a time to Check Your Phone

On days where I find myself too addicted to my phone, I tell myself that after every hour of work, I will take out 10 minutes to check the feed. This works great because I tend to work harder because the associated reward at the end is what I truly desire. Moreover, since I have convinced my mind that freedom is just around the corner, I am better able to focus on the task at hand.

Disable notifications

Someone liked your photo, followed you back, retweeted your tweet, shared or commented on your status are all the things that happen every day. The worst part, you get a notification on your phone every time any of that happens and the little bugger of blue light keeps blinking until you address it. The moment you hear the buzz or beep, your mind becomes distracted. It takes Zen levels of concentration to resist the temptation to check it. Therefore, for your peace of mind, disable the app's notifications from your phone.

Delete the app

Okay, this may seem cruel but it is a necessity these days. We already run short on time with all that we have to accomplish, adding an app or two and engaging in them for hours shouldn't cut it. On days when you have to work your ass off and meet a deadline, I suggest that you delete the app from your phone altogether. You will still have your account active on other technological gadgets but achieve better bouts of focus and concentration without them.

Set Offline Rewards

One reason why we find the world of social media too tempting is that we often associate it with some sort of reward in the end. It can be new information, a few likes, and shares, a chat with friends or some inspiration that we had been looking for. The brain seeks pleasure and gets it in any of these forms.

Therefore, if you are trying to limit the interaction on social media, find something rewarding offline so that you are no longer tempted to head back online. Offline rewards can come in the form of hobbies and interests. For instance, if you enjoy playing the guitar or listening to music, do that instead after completing a task. Again, it will keep you driven as the very idea of a reward waiting will make you work faster and smarter.

Chapter 10: Triumphing at Work-Life Balance

You might wonder, why after all those time management tips have I decided to dedicate one whole chapter to just one. Well, doesn't the magician save the best trick for the last? Doesn't a debater end with the greatest argument in the finale? Don't performers drop the mic with a kickass performance as they level up the stages in a reality TV show?

It is because it is the most valuable piece of advice I can offer you. If you have read through the entire book, you must have noticed that rarely have I used the term family or friends in the 18 techniques. It is because, as entrepreneurs, that is what we think of in the last—our families. The people who suffer the most because of our shortcomings. They are the ones who have to blow out the candles on the cake alone after waiting for one parent to come home and celebrate with them. They are the most valued possession one can have—even more valuable than the business, and all the money and fame.

So this final habit on our list of 19 most effective time management strategies is avoiding overindulgence in the world of business. If your ultimate goal is to earn a name for yourself and achieve all your goals, say ten or twenty years from now, you need to know exactly where you are going to be spending your time and how to manage it most effectively.

But is that all we crave from our lives? Is there no room for personal relationships and a life away from your business? Looks like many entrepreneurs face this dilemma. But technically, they aren't to blame entirely. Hey, I am not just trying to give them an easy pass, here. Let's take a look at their journey to becoming an entrepreneur to understand better.

When you start, you are startled by how many people dream of owning a business but never actually go after their dreams. So you tell yourself that you won't be like them and not waste your talent, ideas, and capabilities. Then you learn how many businesses fail in the first year of their establishment so you tell yourself that you won't be like them and thus work harder toward your goals. You begin working harder than everyone.

Then you finally start making profits and face the real entrepreneurial challenges that make you realize that only the smartest can continue. So you put in more effort, hire more people, then hire some more people to manage them and so on. In the meanwhile, you neglect your family and friends because you are mostly working overtime and managing a bigger staff than you initially started with, causing you to stress more. There is this ever-present guilt of not spending time with your kids and family, and it just keeps piling onto the stress.

And family isn't the only thing that we all need. We also need rest, vacation, and love.

This is where work-life balance comes in.

What Does Work-Life Balance Mean?

A work-life balance means management of your work in such a way that the non-work aspects don't get neglected. Meaning, we must strive to find a balance in our lives and work without compromising on any of those. Entrepreneurs rate this as the topmost worry that they face. Some work for 60+ hours per week, leaving very little time for other activities such as taking care of your health, getting a good night's sleep and spending time with our loved ones.

Why Work-Life Balance is Crucial?

Maintenance of a balance between your work and personal life is important for several reasons. For starters, it affects our health and burns us out.

Working for long hours every day is bound to affect your health physically. It drains your mind, leads to physical strain and is accompanied by bad sleeping habits. Secondly, there is no proven way to tell whether you worked for longer hours or not. Of course, you might notice the physical changes right away but how can you say that working for long hours means more work? After all, everyone's attention and focus span are different. Some might take over a task and complete it in an hour. Someone with the same task may take two or three hours for it.

Finally, and most importantly, it is your relationships that suffer the most. Just your presence in the house isn't important. What is the point of staying glued to your laptop even during your off hours from work? The kids or your spouse won't find you of any use, and this usually results in an ever-increasing gap between the two of you. Most of us are working this hard so that we can provide our families with the best, but is it only our money that they need? Long working hours can negatively affect the well-being, communication, and functioning of your family, so you have to stop right there.

To help you overcome the ever-present urge to be connected with your business at all times, continue reading below.

How to Create Equilibrium between your Work and Personal Relationships?

- Allot separate time for the family and work. Don't bring your work home or your family to your work.
- Develop a list of priorities that also include your family.
- Delegate tasks that can be handled by your manager or employees so that you can have more time to work upon your relationships and health.
- Don't ignore your health and have at least seven hours of sleep every night to allow your brain some time to recharge.
- If there are any menial items on your priority list that can be eliminated or postponed to another date, do that. Use that free time to spend with your friends or family.
- Be strategic and strict with your time. If the clock tells you it's time to pack up and leave one, don't deliberately try to delay leaving, thinking you can accomplish so much more.
- List your priorities on a calendar or in a planner. Plan the activities of the whole week ahead of time so that by the weekend, you are free to go and visit

places with your family.

- Make promises that you can deliver. Don't act as a big show in front of the clients by promising them tight deadlines. Give yourself enough room so that you have time for some emergency or contingency work and don't fall short of them.
- Listen to the needs of your body. If you have been yawning for the past five minutes, consider it a sign and go to bed. What's the point of earning all that money when your health is at risk?

Conclusion

Time Management is the real deal and yet many entrepreneurs fail to comprehend its imperativeness. Time is a priceless asset and not being able to use it to your advantage only means that you aren't that good of an entrepreneur anyway. It sounds like a big thing to say, but I have personally witnessed the struggle of many aspiring entrepreneurs thinking they have what it takes to start a new venture and fall hard on the group. The money is no longer in the bag, the idea that had the potential to grow is open to the public and we all know how it goes from there. The burden of failure that never leaves your mind is enough to drown you into regrets.

Benjamin Franklin was clearly in his right mind when he said, "One today is worth two tomorrows. Lost time is never found again. Time is money. Dost thou love life? Then do not squander time, for that's the stuff that life is made of. You may delay, but time will not." (Franklin, n.d.)

Even if you just focus on one aspect of that, "Time is money," you can summarize the entire book in those three ordinary words put together to form a universal philosophy for making money that no one in the entire world can argue with.

Let's revisit what we learned together in the book for one last time. This time, only with more determination that you will follow and use these to address your time-related concerns and learn to manage it more effectively.

We started with how procrastination affects even the smartest of minds and leaves them barren from all creativity and focus. We then moved on to comprehending how finishing the most important tasks of the day first thing in the morning can lift off the greatest stress and the inspiration and positive reinforcement helps you tackle some more.

Then inhabit 3 and 4, we discussed in great depth the benefits of having an inbox zero and later learned of how to handle and respond to incoming emails. In the same chapter, we also learned how sometimes saying no to favors and opportunities can pave way for better ones in the end and why the need for overburdening yourself with more work and promises isn't indispensable.

In chapter 3, we focused on dealing with time wasters and how we can reprogram our schedules to make space for that 20 % of things with 80% value. Then we deliberated onto the benefits of starting the day early as well as for opting for a healthy and nutritious diet to ensure maximum levels of productivity.

Moving on, we saw how important delegation of tasks is in today's world and also the need for having a clutter-free space and mind to promote task completion and minimize distractions.

Next, we learned about the importance of scheduling as well as task prioritization—two of the most crucial habits to adopt and live by. Both of these habits help you build a roadmap where every stop has been marked. It makes handling of tasks not only possible but also makes it enjoyable.

Then in chapter 7, we looked at how moving past the failures is the way to run a business and crying over missed opportunities isn't fruitful in any way. We also learned how to use single-tasking to reach goals with a clear head and maximum throughput.

Following that, in chapter 8 we identified the root causes of overspending time on any given tasks and how that can be utilized elsewhere. In the same chapter, we also discussed the differences between a goals vs. dreams to-do list and which one to focus more on.

Past that, we learned of the benefits of disconnecting from social media and how to not become an addict as well as how we can all benefit from a stress-free work environment.

In the final chapter, we learned of the importance and values of work-life balance and how you can find one.

What I want you to take away from this book isn't the wisdom but the truth. The truth of how the management of time can affect you positively and enhance your processes to achieve the goals you have set for yourself. I want you all to learn that management of time helps improve all aspects of your work and not just your personal development. The more punctual and determined you are toward your goals, so will your employees be. Set a good example for them to follow and help your enterprise compete with the giants in your industry in no time.

Works Cited

Currey, M. (2013). Daily Rituals: How Artists Work . Knopf .

(2015). Email Statistics Report, 2015-2019. The Radicati Group, Inc. .

Eerde, W. V. (2016). Procrastination and Well-Being at Work. Procrastination, Health, and Well-Being, 233–253. doi: 10.1016/b978-0-12-802862-9.00011-6

Gage, D. (2012, September 20). The Venture Capital Secret: 3 Out of 4 Start-Ups Fail. Retrieved from The Wall Street Journal: https://www.wsj.com/articles/SB100008723963 90443720204578004980476429190

Grant, A. (n.d.). Adam Grant Quotes. Retrieved from Brainy Quotes: https://www.brainyquote.com/quotes/adam_gra nt_834231

Hampton, K., Rainie, L., Lu, W., Shin, I., & Purcell, K. (2015). Psychological Stress and Social Media Use. Pew Research Center.

Katz, I., Eilot, K., & Nevo, N. (2014). "I'll do it later": Type of motivation, self-efficacy and homework procrastination. Motivation and Emotion, 111–119.

Matthews, K. (2014, September 4). Your Office Isn't Big Enough for Clutter and Productivity. Retrieved from Entrepreneur: https://www.entrepreneur.com/article/237081

McCrea, S. M., Liberman, N., Trope, Y., & Sherman, S. J. (2008). Construal Level and Procrastination. Psychological Science, 1308–1314.

McMains, S., & Kastner, S. (2011). Interactions of Top-Down and Bottom-Up Mechanisms in Human Visual Cortex. Journal of Neuroscience, 587-597.

O'Brien, P. D., Hinder, L. M., Callaghan, B. C., & Feldman, D. L. (2017). Neurological consequences of obesity. The Lancet Neurology, 465-477.

OTT, B., & BADAL , S. B. (2015). Delegating: A Huge Management Challenge for Entrepreneurs. BUSINESS JOURNAL.

Piers, S. (2007). The nature of procrastination: A meta-analytic and theoretical review of quintessential self-regulatory failure. Psychological Bulletin, 65-94.

Potkewitz, H. (2016). Why 4 a.m. Is the Most Productive Hour. The Wall Street Journal.

Pychyl , T. A., & Flett, G. L. (2012). Procrastination and Self-Regulatory Failure: An Introduction to the Special Issue. Journal of Rational-Emotive & Cognitive-Behavior Therapy, 203–212.

Sarris, J., Logan, A. C., Akbaraly, T. N., Amminger, G. P., Freeman, M., Hibbiln, J., & Nanri, A. (2015). Nutritional medicine as mainstream in psychiatry. The Lancet Psychiatry, 71-274.

Tibbetta, T. P., & Ferrarib, J. R. (2015). The portrait of the procrastinator: Risk factors and results of an indecisive personality. Personality and Individual Differences, 175-184.

References:

10 Big Differences Between Goals and Dreams That You Must Know. (2013, April 15). Retrieved from https://timemanagementninja.com/2013/04/10-big-differences-between-goals-and-dreams-that-you-must-know/.

7 Reasons to Keep the Inbox Empty. (2017, July 26). Retrieved from https://www.aim.com.au/blog/7-reasons-keep-inbox-empty.

Castrillon, C. (2019, April 8). How Entrepreneurs Can Just Say No. Retrieved from https://www.forbes.com/sites/carolinecastrillon/2019/04/07/how-entrepreneurs-can-just-say-no/#125b16cf7595.

Council, Y. E. (2019, January 28). 7 Tips to Overcome Regret Over Missed Opportunities. Retrieved from https://www.inc.com/young-entrepreneur-council/change-your-mindset-stop-dwelling-on-past-mistakes-with-these-7-tips.html.

Deal With Time Wasters for Effective Time Management. (n.d.). Retrieved from https://www.streetdirectory.com/travel_guide/1

84071/human_resources/deal_with_time_waste
rs_for_effective_time_management.html.

Fight Entrepreneurial Procrastination. (2017,
January 5). Retrieved from
https://startupmindset.com/fight-
entrepreneurial-procrastination/.

Fitzpatrick, J. (2013, June 24). A Case for
Singletasking: The One-Task-At-a-Time Method.
Retrieved from https://lifehacker.com/a-case-
for-singletasking-the-one-task-at-a-time-
method-5646560.

Hazlewood, T. (2019, September 23). The case for
maintaining a singular focus. Retrieved from
https://medium.com/swlh/the-case-for-
maintaining-a-singular-focus-8344ed9d09e.

Heyne, A. (2014, December 10). 5 Ways Being
Healthier Makes Entrepreneurs More Successful.
Retrieved from
https://www.lifehack.org/articles/lifestyle/5-
ways-being-healthier-makes-entrepreneurs-
more-successful.html.

Jaffe, E. (n.d.). Why Wait? The Science Behind
Procrastination. Retrieved from
https://www.psychologicalscience.org/observer/
why-wait-the-science-behind-procrastination.

Kashyap, V. (2018, April 24). 6 things you must do to build an ideal work environment. Retrieved from https://medium.com/@kashyapvartika/6-things-you-must-do-to-build-an-ideal-work-environment-75070638c097.

Kolowich, L. (n.d.). The Productivity Diet: What to Eat to Get More Done in a Day [Infographic]. Retrieved from https://blog.hubspot.com/marketing/productivity-diet.

Kulkarni, C. (2018, July 12). How to Say 'No' More Often: Why Every Entrepreneur Needs a 'To-Don't' List. Retrieved from https://www.entrepreneur.com/article/312732.

MacKay, J. (2019, July 19). How to Prioritize Work: 7 Practical Methods for When "Everything is Important". Retrieved from https://blog.rescuetime.com/how-to-prioritize/.

Marshall, P. (2013, November 8). The 80/20 Rule of Time Management: Stop Wasting Your Time. Retrieved from https://www.entrepreneur.com/article/229813.

Mattperman. (2019, February 27). How to Get Your Email Inbox to Zero Every Day. Retrieved from https://www.whatsbestnext.com/2008/11/how-to-get-your-email-inbox-to-zero-every-day/.

McCann, J. (2018, January 25). Entrepreneurs Need To Pay More Attention To Work-Life Balance -- Here's How. Retrieved from https://www.forbes.com/sites/forbestechcouncil/2018/01/25/entrepreneurs-need-to-pay-more-attention-to-work-life-balance-heres-how/#4dce34246b33.

Rampton, J. (2015, January 28). The Best Ways to Manage Time Wasters. Retrieved from https://www.inc.com/john-rampton/best-way-to-manage-time-wasters.html.

Rampton, J. (2018, November 30). Why People Who Schedule Fewer Tasks Get More Done. Retrieved from https://www.entrepreneur.com/article/324045.

Raza, A. (2017, February 11). 3 Ways the Work Environment Defines the Entrepreneur. Retrieved from https://www.entrepreneur.com/article/287712.

Schwantes, M. (2016, August 25). Want to Boost Productivity? Start Your Mornings at This Ungodly Hour. Retrieved from https://www.inc.com/marcel-schwantes/4-am-morning-most-productive-time-of-day.html.

Vanderbloemen, W. (2016, February 2). How Successful People Start Their Day. Retrieved from https://www.forbes.com/sites/williamvanderbloemen/2016/01/31/how-successful-people-start-their-day/#5eec1b31726e.

Wolf, K. (2017, March 23). Minimize Your Email Inbox to Maximize Productivity. Retrieved from https://redbooth.com/blog/tame-the-email-beast-minimize-your-email-inbox-to-maximize-your-productivity.